KNIGHT-CAPRON LIBRARY
LYNCHBURG COLLEGE
LYNCHBURG, VIRGINIA 24501

WITHDRAWN

MAJOR INDIAN NOVELS

Major Indian Novels

An Evaluation

Edited by
N. S. Pradhan

HUMANITIES PRESS

HUMANITIES PRESS INC
Atlantic Highlands
New Jersey 07716

ISBN 0 391 03409 X

© N. S. Pradhan
First Published, 1986

Printed in India.

CONTENTS

Introduction	vii
1. R.K. Dhawan MULK RAJ ANAND: *Coolie*	1
2. Vasant A. Shahane RAJA RAO: *Kanthapura*	22
3. Harish Trivedi AHMED ALI: *Twilight in Delhi*	41
4. N.K. Jain KAMLA MARKANDAYA: *Nectar in a Sieve*	74
5. Prafulla C. Kar KHUSHWANT SINGH: *Train to Pakistan*	88
6. Suresh Raichura R.K. NARAYAN: *The Guide*	104
7. N.S. Pradhan MANOHAR MALGONKAR: *A Bend in the Ganges*	135
8. Ramesh K. Srivastava BHABANI BHATTACHARYA: *Shadow from Ladakh*	155
9. Devinder Mohan ARUN JOSHI: *The Foreigner*	174
10. Brijraj Singh RUTH PRAWER JHABVALA: *Heat and Dust*	192

11. Lakhmir Singh
    CHAMAN NAHAL: *Azadi*   223
12. Malashri Lal
    ANITA DESAI: *Fire on the Mountain*   242
    Notes on the Contributors   263

INTRODUCTION

Major Indian Novels is yet another addition to the numerous studies, of which there has been an impressive array in the last two decades, on the subject of the Indian novel written in English. R.K. Srinivasa Iyengar's *Indian Writing in English* (1962) was the first major wide-ranging survey that not only took notice of the nineteenth century beginnings and the subsequent growth of this literature, it also took up cudgels against those who ridiculed Indian writing in English ('Matthew Arnold in a Sari' was how Indian poetry in English was described by an English critic!). In his gentle yet firm voice Iyengar said that Indo-Anglian literature was "a tree that has sprung up on hospitable soil from a seed that a random breeze had brought from afar."[1] C.D. Narasimhaiah in *The Swan and the Eagle* (1969) which is mainly a detailed study of three major Indian novelists viz., Mulk Raj Anand, R.K. Narayan and Raja Rao, concluded that their "essentially Indian sensibility" had arisen out of a happy conjunction of the Swan (East) and the Eagle (West). He particularly noticed the quality of "inwardness" which the Indian writers had achieved while writing in the English language. Referring largely in the same vein to the "two parent traditions", Meenakshi Mukherjee's *The Twice Born Fiction* (1971) contains perhaps the most competent study to-date of the major themes in the Indo-Anglisn novel of the last fifty years or so. *Critical Essays on Indian Writing in English* (1972) edited by M.K. Naik, S.K. Desai and G.S. Amur offered the first major collection of essays on a variety of aspects of this literature.

Among the more recent publications, R.S. Singh's *Indian Novel in English* (1977), Raji Narasimhan's controversial *Sensibility Under Stress* (1976), Meenakshi Mukherjee's (ed.) *Considerations* (1977), R.K. Dhawan's (ed.) *Explorations in Modern Indo-English Fiction* (1982) and M.K. Naik's *Dimensions of Indian English Literature* (1984) may be mentioned as having kept the focus on the Indian novel in English. The Writers Worshop, Calcutta has also brought out several good publications relating to this area of literature. Undoubtedly, these critical studies have not only depicted the emergence and flowering of the Indo-Anglian (by now a popular, well-accepted, nomenclature) literature, they have imparted to it well-deserved recognition and status.

Although Indian writing in English began in the mid-nineteenth century, it came into its own only in the third decade of the twentieth century, simultaneously with, and in a sense arising out of, the Gandhian movement and the struggle for India's independence. Almost instantaneously, this literature began to project the themes of patriotism, social justice, East-West confrontation, rural-urban conflict, family relations, etc. Further, although the literary scene was largely dominated in the earlier stages by the

Introduction

three 'giants', Mulk Raj Anand, R.K. Narayan and Raja Rao, a younger generation of bolder and more experimental novelists, several of whom are women, has taken over whose works promise a new sensibility and a vibrant richness.

Unfortunately, and quite needlessly, some of the earlier critics were engaged in a prolonged 'language' controversy. V.Y. Kantak asked (and answered in the affirmative) whether Indian novelists could successfully express themselves in a 'foreign' language or if they could create the 'feel' of life in an 'alien' medium.[2] Raji Narasimhan drew attention to the 'basic unnaturalness' of the Indians writings in English. Other commentators maintained that the Indian novelists could do so successfully as long as "the operative sensibility of the writer is essentially *Indian*"[3] (emphasis added) or if he drew his artistic sustenance from his heritage by choosing a "specifically Indian subject-matter" and by projecting an Indian 'ethos'. The emphasis behind this line of thinking involves three critical assumptions: that English is an 'alien' medium in which the Indian writer may not be able to express himself 'naturally'; that he can do so only if he emphasizes his 'Indianness'; and that this Indianness implicitly stands at variance with or in a dialectical relationship with the element of the 'west' in their culture.

It is submitted that all these three assumptions are erroneous, misleading and, to some extent, dangerous since they tend to make Indo-Anglian literature apologetic, restrictive and parochial. Whereas the view about the 'foreigness' of English has since long been repudiated and dismissed (Iyengar: "English is but one of the languages in which India speaks."[4]), the other two notions need to be sorted out in order that the Indo-Anglian literature may be written and enjoyed by having itself rid of its negative connotations. In this context, it may be fruitful to refer to two authentic literary voices who have sounded the alert about these pitfalls. Referring to the 'inescapable' presence of the East-West theme in most of the Indo-Anglian writing, A.N. Kaul appropriately cautions against an exaggerated projection of this theme which ends up by being 'unreal', 'fabricated' and 'overt'[5]. A sterner warning comes from T.D. Brunton who regards the element of the so-called 'Indianness' as 'sterile' as it places a "premium on eccentricity and freakish originality." For him "fake profundity, orientalism and lush scene-painting" are some of the avoidable attributes of an 'Indian' novel.[6]

The twelve essays of this volume, on novels written by Indians in English, have been especially written with a common purpose: to choose a representative work and to provide an in-depth discussion leading to an overview of the novelist and thus bring together in one volume the kind of material one finds scattered only in journals. One could find fault with the choice of novels and for instance, maintain, with undeniable logic, that *The Serpent and the Rope*, *The Untouchable* or *He Who Rides a Tiger* should have been given preference over the novels chosen. Also arguable is the exclusion of 'major' novels like *All About H.*

Hatter or the inclusion of *Heat and Dust*, many people being of the view that Jhabvala is not an Indo-Anglian writer. There is no real defense against these and similar other possible criticisms. The scholars were simply invited to choose their authors and decide upon the most 'representative' novel. The outcome, it is sincerely hoped, may give to the graduate student better range and depth in his study of the novels and may unfold to the research scholar some fresh insights and perspectives.

Notes

1. K.R. Srinivasa Iyengar, *Indian Writing in English*. (New Delhi: Asia Publishing House), 1962, p. 15.
2. V.Y. Kantak: "The Language of Indian Fiction in English" in *Critical Essays on Indian Writing in English*, ed. Naik, Desai, Amur (Dharwar: Karnatak University Press), 1972, p.221.
3. R.S. Pathak: "The Indo-English Novelists' Quest for Identity" in *Explorations in Modern Indo-English Fiction*, ed. R.K. Dhawan (New Delhi: Bahri Publications), 1982, p.4.
4. K.R. Srinivasa Iyengar, p. 3.
5. A.N. Kaul: "R.K. Narayan and the East-West Theme" in *Considerations*, ed. Meenakshi Mukherjee (New Delhi: Allied Publishers), 1977, p. 45.
6. T.D. Brunton. "India in Fiction: The Heritage of Indianness" in *Critical Essays on Indian Writing in English,* Naik, Desai & Amur, p. 200.

MULK RAJ ANAND: *Coolie*

R.K. Dhawan

"Among the Indo-English novelists," observes Anniah Gowda, "Mulk Raj Anand is the most conspicuously committed writer.... Perhaps the best word for it is the plainest: it is propaganda writing."[1] The propaganda novel in the true sense is one so dominated by its author's ulterior purpose that the propaganda cannot be ignored, and normally one who disliked that line of propaganda would find the book unreadable. Such a novel, Gowda opines, cannot rank among the great works of literature. In a similar vein, Chetan Karnani complains of the extra-literary intentions of the novelist: "The trouble with Anand is that he is not able to hide his proletarian sympathies."[2] These 'determined' detractors of Anand, and some others, charge him of having used the artistic medium of the novel for pure propaganda; indoctrination, they hold, does not go with the creative process and aesthetic experience.

Anand is not deterred by such criticism: "I do not in the least mind criticism, even adverse, probably because the suffering from which my novels have been written has already been rewarded by the fact that they have gone into so many languages of the world in spite of their truthfulness and exposure of the many shams, hypocrisies and orthodoxies of India."[3] This is true, for in his fiction Anand was heeding his artistic conscience than following any pre-conceived formula. And that accounts for the abiding appeal of his novels. What is merely purposive inside a coterie and sensational with the transient turmoils which it depicts cannot hope to endure unless it holds a core of eternal, universal truth.

In this respect *Coolie*, published some fifty years ago, is perhaps the best of Anand's novels; it is contemporary, naturalistic, topical and in harmony with the prevailing English literary mood. No wonder, then, that it obtained an extensive readership in several countries and was acclaimed as one of the best-known socially-realistic novels of the nineteen-thirties. It demonstrates an early tendency in Anand to present life in terms of proletarian experience. "As a total novel of human experience," writes Anand, "*Coolie* does not need special pleading. It sweeps the reader along on the curve of its essential force . . . as well as its fundamentalism."[4]

Anand vigorously affirms his position as a social realist: "I am not in the least frightened of the charges of propaganda. . . The novel *(Coolie)* is integral. It has a life quality about it, almost as if the pages got fire from the frame of the tragic hero."[5] Taking a strong dig at the Indian critics, he observes: ". . . nobody in the many languages into which *Coolie* has gone has suggested that it is propaganda, except some Indian critics who . . . regard contemporary themes, especially from the lower depths, as extra-literary material. . . . And oddly enough, they take refuge behind the categories of Western academic criticism and dismiss anything about raw life as 'naturalism' or 'realism' or 'social realism'. They will accept Tolstoy and Dickens and Hardy, but should an Indian try to portray the peasants of India, or slum children, or the maid servants, you are written off as a 'communist propagandist'."[6]

Coolie, as also other early writings of Anand, cannot be fully appreciated unless studied in relation to the movement of the nineteen-thirties in Western Europe. For as a writer he was shaped in the thirties when several problems were more important than the individual; the problem, then, that Anand "tried to face as a writer was not strictly a private, but a private-public problem."[7] As it was, he found it impossible to maintain aloofness from politics in the post-World War Europe.

Anand stayed in London for over two decades, from 1924 to 1945; he was therefore deeply influenced by the Progressive Movement in literature that flourished in the thirties. In London, Anand came under numerous literary, political and social influences and it is in them that the sources of his synthesis of Marxist and humanist thought can be seen. "You will find that amorphous as my books are'" writes Anand, "I did stick to the novel form, more or less, as an imaginative interpretation of Indian life rather than use it as a vehicle to sermonise. And the posing of the problems of human beings in the 30's by people like Malraux, Celine and Hemingway gave the necessary sense of discrimination to my own treatment of the predicament of our people as against the European view."[8] He was an overt nationalist and championed the socialist cause in his fiction in common with many European and American writers of the day.

The peculiar conditions during the early decades of the century in Europe and elsewhere put a great pressure on the writers to sympathise with the socialist cause. The complacency following the the First World War, based on the erroneous belief that the League of Nations was going to preserve peace and security, was suddenly exploded, leaving a feeling of loss and disenchantment. There was a complete erosion of human values.

Another event that had a profound influence on writers like Anand was the general strike of 1926 in Great Britain. It made them conscious of the class war between haves and have-nots in modern civilization. On his arrival in England, Anand had admired Britain for its achievements in science and technology. Living through the strike, this illusion of his was shattered with a bang. He increasingly came to realize that the scientific and technological discoveries if controlled by a select band of people need not result in social benefits. "And it was no use speculating on the beneficences of science," avers Anand, "if its discoveries were to be manipulated to their own advantage by a small group of individuals who controlled the key industries and had an absolute say in matters of domestic and foreign policy."[9]

The object of the General Strike was to attain specific rights for the mine workers; in a way it was a proletarian challenge to the government and its capitalist bias. Anand and a group of his colleagues sided with the workers; they felt dismayed at the failure of the strike. The strike had revealed the reactionary character of the English State "that it could put back human progress for a thousand years."[10] Anand felt convinced "that the people of Britain, no less than the people of India, had yet to win their liberty."[11]

After the destruction wrought by the first World War, European society had plunged anew into the shadows of economic depression and cynical mood. The economic depression caused disastrous effects; it gave rise to unemployment that brought in its fold unending distress and appalling misery.

The rise of Fascism in Italy under Mussolini and the Nazi power in Germany in 1933 under Hitler reflected the paralysis of the Western democracies. The Japanese aggression on Manchuria in 1931, the Italian rape of Ethiopia in 1935, the extinction of Spanish Republic at the hands of Germany and Italy in 1936-37, all in succession tolled the death knell of the League of Nations.

Such a disintegrating world disillusioned the intellectual of the day; he strove for a commitment that would restore order and save his world from the existing chaos. The writer was not only absorbing the atmosphere as a participant but also seemed readily inclined to reflect it in his writing.

Alarmed at the situation, the intellectuals of the West prominently led by Maxim Gorky of Russia, Roman Rolland of France, Thomas Mann of Germany, and E.M. Forster of England assembled in Paris in 1935. They raised the voice of liberty as Shelley and Dickens had done in their own times. "I want greater freedom for writers," declared Forster, "both as creators and critics for the . . . maintenance of culture."[12] He appealed to the writers to be courageous and sensitive to fulfil their 'public calling'; he urged them to come forward and arouse the people to act and struggle for creating a just and humane society. The conference was dominated by the writers possessing socialist background, or having some affiliations with communism. They posed a premonition of a threatening situation, caused by the aggressive imperialism of the day. The psychology working in the background was the moving force that impelled the writers to use their talents against fascism and write for the working classes.

Inspired by these ideas some Indian students studying in England assembled in London a few months after the Paris Conference and formed Progressive Writers Association. Their meetings were attended and occasionally addressed by Ralph Fox, Karnford and Caudwell. They framed a manifesto of the Association which was fina-

Coolie

lized, amongst others, by Mulk Raj Anand and Sajjad Zaheer.[13]

The progressive writers believed that the principal function of literature was to reflect and express the aspirations and fundamental problems of the toiling masses and ultimately help in the formation of a socialist society. Even those who were not Marxists adhered to the idea of a basic social transformation and political independence. A new content is discerned in literature which not only bears out a radically revolutionary character but also a basically new rationale for such a change. "That truth alone should matter to a writer," says Anand in his essay "Why I Write?", "that this truth should become imaginative truth without losing sincerity. The novel should interpret the truth of life, from *felt experience,* and not from books."[14]

The Progressive Movement then was a reaction against the esoteric and inward-looking art of the nineteen-twenties. In England, it began with the publication of Michael Robert's anthologies, *New Signatures and New Country* which grouped Auden, Spender, Day Lewis, Isherwood and Edward Upward together for the first time. These writers were responsible for making social realism and tendentious literature of revolt fashionable in both Europe and America. It was during the same time that Anand was working on his novel *Coolie*. He essentially shared the political and social philosophy of the left wing intellectuals: "there was ample confirmation in the thinking aloud of the younger writers like Aragon, Malarux, Auden, Spender, Day Lewis and others that the questions they were asking themselves were more or less similar to ours in India, and, irrespective of race and colour, we shared similar concepts and aspired towards kindred objects."[15] *Left Review,* an important organ of the new writers, carried extracts from the then unpublished *Coolie.*

The particular conditions of the thirties account for many close resemblances between Anand and George Orwell; both had much in common: a passionate sense of social injustice, "a recognition, more than a recognition, indeed knowledge—of the innumerable frustrations and suppressions. Both men hated the social prejudices that helped to maintain the oppressive status quo; the class system in England, the caste system in India."[16] Moreover, both the writers shared a profound dislike of colonialism. Orwell and Anand both proved their readiness to act in support of their political convictions by getting in the Civil War in Spain. In tone and temper, Orwell's *Road to Wigan Pier* carries the same burden as Anand's *Coolie.*

One of the notable consequences of this movement was a growing rejection of the aesthetic theory of 'art for art's sake.' Anand has felt, from the very initial stages of his awareness of the human predicament, that the writer cannot shut himself in an ivory tower; he cannot stand on a high perch, but has to go into the raging storm itself, to be with the people, to ally himself with their many sorrows and little joys. The purpose of the novel, according to Anand, is to change mankind, and through mankind society. He is vehemently opposed to the formalists or aesthetes who hold that art, though influenced by life, is essentially governed by its inner logic and not by outside forces.[17] Nor has he any sympathy with the writers who are self-centred subjectivists indulging merely in petty variations of Proustian aestheticism.

The thirties movement defined in specific terms the position of the artist and the functions of his art. In *Apology for Heroism,* Anand places the writer on a very high pedestal, glorifying him as "precisely the man who can encompass the whole of life."[18] He is superior to the moralist, the scientist and the politician, each of whom takes a limited view of man, while the writer "is uniquely fitted to aspire to be a whole man, to attain, as far as possible, a more balanced perspective of life."[19] A novelist like any other artist is concerned chiefly with the truth. And he reveals it not like the philosopher who does it in a cold statement of dogma but only in terms of life, rendered through the devices of dramatization.

Anand, like Lawrence, Gorky, and Eric Gill, believes that the work of a genuine creative writer is inspired by a mission. He seems to be in full agreement with Arnold's dictum that literature at bottom is the criticism of life. He is strongly committed to his creed, and in his opinion "any writer who said that he was not interested in *la condition humaine* was either posing or yielding to a fanatical love of isolationism—a perverse and clever defence of the adolescent desire to be different."[20]

The thirties movement proved to be a watershed in the literary sensibility in Europe. It shook the writers from age-old slumber and awakened them to the realization of new possibilities which had so far eluded them. The early fiction of Anand was truly representative of the movement. His fictional world depicted not the feudal splendours and mysticism of traditional Indian literature, but the hard and suffering lives of the millions of his countrymen. Anand deserves credit for establishing the novel as a favoured medium for Indo-English writers and for deflecting the literature from a worn-out romantic poetising into the move vigorous forms of realistic prose-fiction.

In the choice of themes, therefore, Anand is unquestionably an innovator. He is the first novelist writing in English to choose as his raw material the lower-class life of the Indian masses. In *The Untouchable* and *Coolie*, he almost dreads the flight of imagination, feels shy of soaring high and keeps close to the ground with a vengeance. He does not hesitate to turn the floodlight on the darkest spots in Indian life.

Coolie is a proletarian novel as it focuses on the predicament of the underprivileged; it narrates the miserable life of a labourer or a coolie. The satire is directed against the iniquitous injustice of Indian society which treats servants as servile creatures and outcasts. More than that, it brings into sharp focus the capitalist domination and the role of

Coolie

money as a key factor in all spheres of life. This is what Munoo, the central character of *Coolie*, learns in his short life.

Anand has always felt that the less privileged populations in a country like India have been deliberately kept at a level of sub-humanity. In *Apology for Heroism*, he bemoans the plight of the coolies. "It never seemed to have entered tha heads of our masters," says Anand, "to give the coolies the slightest chance of bettering themselves. They were supposed to be sub-human. They worked from dawn to dusk, old and young, male and female, for their masters, and they were treated like dogs."[2][1]

Coolie has an epical sweep; Munoo represents specific phases of proletarian existence in specific settings. The novel is dexterously divided into five chapters, corresponding to five acts of a tragic play. The first chapter portrays Munoo, the orphan of dispossessed parents, as an innocent little boy in the rural village of Bilaspur in the Kangra hills. The second chapter deals with his tenure as a servant in the household of a bank clerk Babu Nathoo Ram in Sham Nagar. The third chapter recounts his experiences in the feudal city of Daulatpur as a worker in a small pickle factory and as a coolie fighting for work in the city market. The penultimate chapter describes his life as a labourer in Bombay at the British-owned Sir George White Cotton Mills. The last chapter shows him as a servant and rickshaw coolie in the employ of a promiscuous Eurasian, Mrs. Mainwaring, in Simla. In drifting from job to job, from his native hills to the cities of the plain, we get a most vivid panorama of life in India of that period.

Munoo's beginning is typical of the underprivileged class. His father had died a slow death of bitterness and disappointment because he could not pay the interest due to his landlord on the money he had borrowed from him. Munoo could never forget the utter helplessness and tragic destiny of his mother consequent to the death of her husband. Despite the sad memories and the ill-treatment meted out to him by his aunt and uncle, Munoo is happy and contented. Before Munoo leaves his idyllic surroundings in search of earning a livelihood, he is a sensitive and intelligent boy full of animal spirits:

> Munoo was a genius at climbing trees. He would hop on to the trunk like a monkey, climb the bigger branches on all fours, swing himself to the thinner off-shoots as if he were dancing on a trapeze, and then, diving dangerously into space, he would jump from one tree to another.[22]

So, in spite of the fact that his aunt maltreated him and "beat him more than he beat his cattle," (11) he really did not want to go to the town.

Leaving his hills in North-West India, Munoo descends to the plain and becomes a servant in the house of Babu Nathoo Ram, a sub-accountant. The village boy's delight at having come to a colourful city soon vanishes. Bibiji makes his life a hell; she is always ready to hurl filthiest abuses on the innocent boy. He is a mere servant; he has no right to play with other children. He undergoes a dreadful routine of domestic servility; he is made to drudge along from early morning till late in the evening. Once he bursts out weeping before his uncle, complaining about the hard, bitter life he has had since he arrived. Daya Ram silences him by reminding him that he is their servant and so he must not mind what they say.

Munoo frequently thinks over his sad plight and tries to find out the reason of his sufferings:

> "What am I—Munoo?' he asked himself as he lay wrapped in his blanket, early one morning. 'I am Munoo, Babu Nathoo Ram's servant, ' the answer came to his mind.(46)

Munoo does not search for causes and effects. It does not occur to him to ask himself why he is a servant and Babu Nathoo Ram a master. Thoroughly convinced of his inferiority, he accepts his position as a slave, and tries to instil into his own mind the notion of his brutishness, that his mistress has so often nagged him about. And he promises himself that he would be a good servant, a perfect model of a servant.

Munoo's miserable life at the eternally nagging Bibiji's house often makes him contemplate his position in the world. He realizes that money indeed is everything; and his suffering is due to his poverty. Eventually he draws the conclusion: "there must only be two kinds of people in the world: the rich and the poor."(69)

Munoo rebels and runs away from the place ending up in a town called Daulatpur. There he is employed in a pickle factory by the kindly Prabha Dyal and his unscrupulous partner Ganpat. Munoo's lovable nature endears him to Prabha and to Prabha's wife, Parvati. The personal care he receives from them is highly soothing to him. However, very often he feels dismayed and the only thing that "relieved these fits of depression was the silent comradeship which existed between him and the other coolies."(109).

Munoo has to work very hard in the dark suffocating atmosphere in the primitive factory. It is a wretched place where the labourers "worked from day to day in the dark underworld, full of intense heat of blazing furnaces and the dense malodorous smells. . . They worked long hours, from dawn to past midnight, so mechanically that they never noticed the movements of their own or each other's hands " (110). Munoo, the tender boy, leads an infernal life. Things become worse when he is rendered jobless since the factory has closed down because of Ganpat's forgery and treachery in business.

Munoo's sojourn in Bombay as a factory worker provides Anand with an opportunity to describe the pathetic conditions of the workers and their plight in society. A fortuitous meeting with Hari gets Munoo employment in a large British-owned Cotton Mill. Bombay, far from being the land of his heart's desire, proves nightmarish. He is totally disappointed; the poverty and suffering in the city streets appall him. He comes to realize the truth of the statement: "The bigger a city is, the more cruel it is to the sons of Adam... You have to pay even for the breath you breathe" (177). The small and dingy room in which Munoo puts up with eight of his colleagues is nothing short of a living hell.

The Cotton Mills where Munoo comes to work are intended to expose the exploitation of the Indian proletariat by the British imperialists. Munoo here finds himself one of the herd of anonymous workers, cheated and victimized by the English masters. Anand's political alignment with the workers is evidenced as he delineates the harsh lives of the workers and their families, the squalor of the Bombay slums and their exploitation by the moneylenders. The labourers, including wives and children, have long working hours. the wages they get are quite inadequate. The workers are denied even the bare amenities: "There was nowhere for the coolies working in the factory to wash, except at a pump in the grounds... There was nowhere to go for a meal... only a man with two baskets of plain roasted gram and cheap sugar-coated stuff sat outside the factory" (215).

Anand gives a direct and detailed presentation of the socialist programme, which reads like the manifesto of the Progressive Writers' Association of the thirties. Addressing the coolies of the Sirjabite Factory, Sauda, a trade union leader, exhorts them to go on strike in their fight against the employers:

'We are human beings and not soulless machines. ....'

'We want the right to work without having to pay bribes.'

'We want clean houses to live in.'

'We want schools for our children and creches for our babies.'

'We want to be skilled workers.'

'We want to be saved from the clutches of the moneylenders.'

'We want a good wage and no more subsistence allowance if we must go on short work.'

'We want shorter hours.'

'We want security so that the foreman cannot dismiss us suddenly."

'We want our organizations to be recognised by law.'
(226).

Specific settings such as these are used to provoke anger and moral indignation. As a writer of the thirties, Anand's avowed purpose is to treat literature as a social evidence or testimony rather than the literary problem of what happens to the novel when it is subjected to the pressures of politics or political ideology.

The friction between the millowners and the workers has serious repercussions. The strike that erupts from intolerable conditions turns into Hindu-Muslims riots. Bewildered and shocked, Munoo flees from the scene. Before he could jump aside, he is knocked down by the car of Mrs. Mainwaring, a coquettish Anglo-Indian lady. She takes him to Simla and employs him as her personal servant. Munoo moves from place to place with this lecherous lady given to flirting with several men. He has grown into a handsome young fellow and she makes him her rickshaw-puller and lover. This chapter reveals Anand at his bitterest. Munoo, the coolie, is made to carry another human being, a woman at that; and what a woman, "a bitch to all the dogs that prowled round her bungalow" (287). This toilsome work tells severely on Munoo's health and he dies of consumption. His death at the age of sixteen is intended to focus attention on the injustices of society and ills of the economic system.

The novel is a remarkable study of the relation between literature and ideas. In order to make some explicit statements for the cause of the proletariat, Anand chooses to end the novel with a message. For the purpose, he introduces an alter-ego figure, the 'learned' coolie Mohan. He is 'a didactic device'[23] intended to announce the declared 'thesis' of the novel: the evil of a capitalistic social system.

The revolutionary character of his moralizing is revealed when Mohan tells a coolie who has mortgaged his land: "Then come with me, and we shall kill the landlord one day, and get your land" (310). He makes an impassioned appeal for a cooperative system: "It is my object to make you people realise that if you work, you should have a share in the things that you produce with the sweat of your brow" (310). The coolies fail to understand him.

"You will let them kill you," bursts out Mohan, "you are all ignorant slaves. How can I drill any sense into your heads " (310). The efforts of Mohan will not go in vain; for, in the recreation of the coolie and his despicable existence Anand has stirred up the human in every reader.

Anand's critique of the Indian society in the novel follows recognisably socialist thought, though socialism is strongly blended with humanitarian zeal. His preoccupation with contemporary issues and his faith in humanistic ideals are best reflected in the course of the narrative. *Coolie* not only reveals Anand at his best but also provides ample material for examining his treatment of artistic problems facing the Indo-English novelist in the nineteen-thirties. It seeks to present a vivid panorama of life in India; it is propagandist in the sense that any frank statement of facts is bound to appeal for their correctness. In the final count, we must admire Anand's imaginative skill in integrating his sources, and transcending them to produce an intensely realised and credible narrative that is both political thesis and absorbing fiction.

The novelist in the present day cannot abstract himself from the contemporary world; nor can he absolve himself of the role of the seer—one who sees truth and the inner harmony on which the things of life are strung together. He, like Anand, is the Ancient Mariner, and the world the Wedding Guest.

Notes

1. H.H. Anniah Gowda, "Mulk Raj Anand," *The Literary Half-Yearly,* vol. VI, No. 1 (January 1965), p. 50.
2. Chetan Karnani, "Mulk Raj Anand: The Novelist as a Socialist Chronicler", *Thought,* 24 August 1974, p.p. 19—20.
3. Saros Cowasjee, ed., *Author to Critic: The Letters of Mulk Raj Anand to Saros Cowasjee,* Calcutta, 1973, pp. 15—16.
4. *Ibid., p. 18.*
5. *Ibid.,* pp. 21-22.
6. *Ibid.,* p. 22.
7. Mulk Raj Anand, *Apology for Heroism,* Bombay, 1957, p. 78.
8. *Author to Critic,* p. 24.
9. *Apology for Heroism,* p. 32.
10. *Loc, cit.*
11. *Ibid.,* p. 35.
12. E.M. Forster, *Abinger Harvest,* London, 1953, p. 78.
13. Sajjad Zaheer who played a prominent role in the organisation vividly recalls hs association with Anand: "I have had the good fortune of having known Mulk ' . . since 1930, when we were both young and in our twenties and were students in England. During the last years of my stay in England, in 1935, Anand and I, together with a few other young Indians founded

the Indian Progressive Writers' Movement. This was the seed from which developed later in India the great Progressive Writers' Movement, spreading to almost all the great languages of India, blessed and supported by such eminent figures as Tagore and Premchand." *Contemporary Indian Literature*, Vol. V (December 1965), p. 11.

14. Mulk Raj Anand, "Why I Write?," *Kakatiya Journal of English Studies,* Vol. II. No. 1 (Spring 1977) p. 251.
15. *Apology for Heroism*, pp. 79-80.
16. R.K. Dhawan, ed., *Explorations in Modern Indo-English Fiction*, New Delhi, 1982, p. 80.
17. Bhabani Bhattacharya, a contemporary of Anand, holds similar views about the function of literature: "' art for art's sake' is as queer a demand as, say, science for the sake of science. Could the arms, face, or liver of a man claim autonomy in the same manner just because each performed a definite function of its own?" "Literature and Social Reality," *The Aryan Path,* Vol. XXVI (September 1955), p. 394.
18. *Apology for Heroism*, p. 87.
19. *Loc. cit.*
20. *Ibid.*, pp. 81-82.
21. *Apology for Heroism*, p. 74.
22. Mulk Raj Anand, *Coolie*, New Delhi, 1972, p. 12. Other references to this text are indicated by page

numbers in the essay.
23. S.C. Harrex, *The Fire and the Offering*, Calcutta, 1977, p. 87.

RAJA RAO: *Kanthapura*

Vasant A Shahane

Kanthapura (1938) by Raja Rao is a much-acclaimed novel and the grounds for its approbation are fairly well laid out. In his "Author's Foreword" Raja Rao himself has unfolded his central concern in this novel. He writes:

> There is no village in India, however mean, that has not a rich *sthala-purana* or legendary history, of its own. Some god or godlike hero has passed by the village—Rama might have rested under this pipal-tree, Sita might have dried her clothes, after her bath, on this yellow stone, or the Mahatma himself, on one of his many pilgrimages through the country, might have slept in this hut, the low one, by the village gate. In this way the past mingles with the present, and the gods mingle with men to make the repertory of your grand-mother always bright. One such story from the contemporary annals of a village, I have tried to tell [1]

Kanthapura thus becomes a story of an Indian village in Mysore State in the context of its linkage with what is described as a rich *sthala-purana*. The words *sthala-purana* in Sanskrit imply the *purana* of a significant place, the legendary tale of a locale. However, *Kanthapura* is just not one village in the old State of Mysore, it is India in micro-

Kanthapura

cosm. *Kanthapura* is thus particular and general, specific and especial, highly individualistic as well as representative in character, encompassing both the spheres of the regional as well as the universal in the creative writer's cosmos.

Numerous critics of Indo-Anglian fiction have highlighted this quality of *Kanthapura* sometimes by adding extensive summaries which are of course valid and acceptable but none of them to my knowledge has placed their fingers on the weaknesses of *Kanthapura* as a work of the art of fiction.

It is perhaps necessary to present a critical focus on *Kanthapura* in the context of conventional critical categories relevant to it such as the title, the theme, the characters, the plot, the technique of narration etc. before dealing with some of the deeper and more subtle layers of its structure and meaning.

Kanthapura is obviously a place name meaning the abode or habitation of *Kant* (husbands) or *Kanta* (wives), of men and women. It is certainly not *Kantipur,* the town characterised by *Kanti* or radiance since it is shown faced with desolation in the end. Ahmed Ali, a class-mate of Raja Rao, believes that *Kanthapura* "but for its title, would have met with greater success than it did"[2]. The process of Raja Rao gaining his reputation has been rather slow and it took almost two decades before critical opinion appears to have crystallised in acclaiming *Kanthapura* as a minor classic.[3] A few others consider it almost a classic.

It is obvious that the title *Kanthapurs* is not an unmixed blessing, It is both appropriate and odd, meaningful and indistinct in its connotation and its relation to structure and design.

The theme of *Kanthapura* is the continuity of Indian Tradition in a rural setting as well as the political resurgence of the thirties in rural India. *Kanthapura* is a village of simple, lovable, affectionate, generous, talkative, patriotic country-folks nourished on age-long Indian tradition and deeply stirred and activated by the movement for gaining India's freedom from foreign rule. It is amazing that 'Tradition' and this quest for Freedom should go hand in hand, and in fact, be strengthening each other in the social, moral and political contexts of a resurgent India— an India stirred to its roots by the irrepressible spirit and resounding voice of Mahatma Gandhi. Thus the theme of Kanthapura is two-fold: moral-cum-religious, and political. "The inner stream of the novel, though not its whole canvas", writes Ahmed Ali, "concerns Tradition."[4] . Thus, the legendary history of a representative Indian village is brought in close association with its newly gained political consciousness, its deep stirring caused by Gandhi's defiance of the British Imperial power and the movement of non-violent non-cooperation, an effective tool for gaining political freedom.

It has already been stated by critics that the essence, the very soul of *Kanthapura*, lies in its pervasive strand of selfless action, a kind of *Nishkama Karma-Yoga* derived from that great classic of Hindu thought, the *Bhagvad-Geeta* and that this spirit of patriotic and altruistic action is the guiding star of the characters, the source of their inspiration and the spur of their self-sacrifice. The composition of *Kanthapura* obviously coincides with the completion of the early enthusiastic phase of the Gandhian revolutionary activism before disenchantment with the Gandhian ideals set in, and therefore, the men and women in *Kanthapura* are overwhelmingly inspired by the Gandhian passion for freedom and the consequential courage of conviction, of confronting the Raj with non-violent resistance, civil disobedience, and mass movements inspired by these pure and great moral ideals. Gandhi in *Kanthapura* is an invisible rather than an actual presence, his ideas and ideals are made manifest through the character and personality of Moorthy, who is indeed at the centre of the novel's human and political world.

Raja Rao succeeds considerably in outlining and highlighting the 'human geography' of Kanthapura. He achieves his effects through his pictorial power and through the evoking process of his art of scene-making. This portrayal of 'human geography' is an aspect of the novelist's art of landscape painting. Evocative landscapes play a major part in the modern novelist's art of fiction and this is perceptively revealed in the novels of Thomas Hardy, Joseph Conrad, D.H. Lawrence and E.M. Forster. Raja Rao, too, makes a skilful use of his brush to give colour and life to his canvas in *Kanthapura*. Kanthapura is a village situated in the province of Kara (Karnataka?) "high on the Ghats it is", close to the steep mountains facing the Arabian sea, in a fertile land, the valley of the Himavathy, close to the centres of cardamom and coffee, rice and sugar-cane. These products are exported to England and other foreign lands "into the ships the Red-men bring" which go "across the seven oceans" into the countries where our rulers live." (p. 1)

In the first paragraph of the first chapter Raja Rao has not merely outlined the locale of *Kanthapura* but has also voiced the forebodings of the conflict between the red man and the brown-black Indian, the British Imperial power and the patriotically-inspired Moorthy of Kanthapura. The scene-making is precise and vivid and it also unfolds the novel's basic theme.

The second paragraph which concentrates on the movement of carts and 'cartgroans' through the Kanthapura streets, near the Potter's lane, turning at Chennayya's pond and Rama Chetty's house presents essentially a picture of movement—a movement of carts and bullocks, men and coolies which is graphic and suggestive. This movement has a wider significance. It shows that Kanthapura is no longer a static village, it has become dynamic through Moorthy and his men of action and through the consciousness of other village folks. It clearly shows that Kanthapura is on the move and has become resurgent under Mahatma Gandhi's magic spell.

The third paragraph inducts into the picture the image of Goddess Kenchamma:

"Kenchamma is our goddess. Great and bounteous is she. She killed a demon ages, ages ago, a demon that had come to demand our young sons as food and our young women as wives. Kenchamma came from Heaven—it was the sage Tripura who had made penances to bring her down—and she waged such a battle and she fought so many a night that the blood soaked and soaked into the earth, and that is why the Kenchamma Hill is all red. If not, tell me, sister, why should it be red only from the Tippur stream upwards, for a foot down on the other side of the stream you have mud, black and brown but never red. Tell me how could this happen, if it were not for Kenchamma and her battle? Thank heaven, not only did she slay the demon, but she even settled down among us, and this much I shall say, never has she failed us in grief.[5]

Kanthapura, as has been said earlier, is deeply concerned with depicting and highlighting the 'Tradition'. This effect is fully achieved through portraying the temple of village goddess Kenchamma, around which the life and the action, of the heads and hearts, of the villagers seem to revolve. Kenchamma is bounteous and benign as well as destructive of evil, and directed towards the villagers protection. The villagers sing hymns in her honour: "Kenchamma, great Goddess, potect us! O Benign one" (p.3)

The fourth paragraph continues and adds to the depiction of the human geography and landscape of *Kanthapura*. The village comprises twenty-four houses—such as Postmaster Suryanarayana's "double-storied house", Patwari Nanjundaiah's extended house with a verandah and two additional rooms fitted with glass panels, Rangamma's large house (the envy of Waterfall Venkamma) the Figtree-house, Moorthy's corner house etc., etc.. These houses are peopled by men and women whose words and actions breathe life into Kanthapura.

The fifth paragraph describes the caste structure of Kanthapura—an aspect of an age-old (now rather outmoded) tradition. The village is split into the Brahmin quarter, the Potters' quarter, the Weavers' quarter, the Sudra quaarter, the Pariah quarter—the Potters' street once flourishing with houses of prosperity led you to the temple square where Patel Range Gowda had built a 'nine-beamed' house. He had amassed gold just as Bhatta, the rich landowner, had amassed wet lands—this Bhatta who is selfish, wicked, narrow-minded, an opponent of Kanthapura's political resurgence.

The first main motif for action in *Kanthapura* is provided by corner-house Narasamma's son, Moorthy, finding a half-sunk linga and stating: "Why not unearth it and wash it and consecrate it?" "Why not!" said we all—and this event is the starting point of Kanthapura's awakening into a new Gandhian Jerusalem.

Rangamma's learned father, Ramakrishnayya, said "he would read out the *Sankara-Vijaya* day after day". And the Kanthapurians cried out, "May the Goddess bless him" (p. 7) And this started the sermons and explication of the *Vedanta* and the philosophy of *Advaita,* of Sankara, so much so they all celebrated Sankara's *Jayanthi* (p. 7).

Raja Rao puts his finger right on the life-giving nerves of Indian villagers and describes their genuine and instinctive response. They bring in food, flowers, vegetables, oil, camphor, *payasam* (milk mixed with sugar) etc. to celebrate the event. This celebration leads the Kanthapurians to organise other events of similar nature, such as the *Rama-navamy* and *Ganesh Chaturthi* or the holding of *Harikathas* and sermons in the temple-instruments of social change, which though deeply religious in a way, are indeed the major tools of creating political consciousness among the people. The 'human geography' of *Kanthapura* will not be complete unless Moorthy's dynamic movements, spurred by his patriotic ideals are understood and underscored in this novel's progression:

So Moorthy goes from house to house, and from younger brother to elder brother, and from elder brother to the grand-father himself and—what do you think?—he even goes to the Potters' quarter and the Weavers' quarter and the Sudra quarter, and I closed my ears when I heard he went to the Pariah quarter. We said to ourselves, he is one of these Gandhi-men, who say there is neither caste nor clan nor family and yet they pray like us and they live like us. Only they say, too, one should not marry early, one should allow widows to take husbands and a brahmin might marry a pariah and a pariah a brahmin. Well, well, let them say it, how does it affect us? We shall be dead before the world is polluted. We shall have closed our eyes.[6]

Moorthy collects subscriptions from the village folk—a

total of one hundred and forty seven rupees. But these subscriptions are priceless and invaluable as they are indeed tokens of people's strong will to resist the onslaught of the British power and to work towards attaining India's independence.

The first chapter also outlines the story of Creation, of Brahma, Siva and Parvati, the Indian sages and a whole range of cultural tradition. However, the story will not be complete unless it tells the saga of Mahatma Gandhi, a unique figure, an extraordinary leader of men and minds, who created a mass consciousness among Indians about their deplorable bondage and spurred them on to the struggle for regaining their freedom—political, economic and social and create a new society based on Gandhian values—almost an alternative society of high ideals.

Jagannadha Rao, the village Puranik, tells the stories of Gods and Goddesses but these are inextricably linked with the coming of Gandhi on the Indian horizon in *Kanthapura* itself. Thus, the 'tradition' is combined with the new contemporary reality of the India of the thirties and the portrait of the human geography of *Kanthapura* is painted with a powerful brush. The induction of the Gandhian spirit in Kanthapura creates a new wave of enthusiasm, self-help, hard-work, the *charkha*, the spinning wheel distributed free by the Congress organisation through the altruistic Moorthy. This new wave of Gandhian renaissance has many adherents, but it also has staunch opponents such as Bhatta. Bhatta is an embodiment of greed and extreme self-interest. He is indifferent to his family and to his wife, Savithramma, because he has a passion for money. Coins and their sounds exercise a magic spell on him. His unhappy wife dies in an accident and Bhatta marries a teenager. He has become a big land-owner, a zamindar, rather than a mere priest. He indulges in litigation due to his money-lending business and substantially adds to his land holdings. He marries, a real "seven days marriage", followed by sumptuous wedding feasts. "Never have one seen a marriage like Bhatta's. Such *Pheni*. After all a Zamindar's house, my sister!" (p.23). Bhatta, however, has some redeeming features. He is not a totally dark character. He helps a young man from Kanthapura to complete his education and find a good position in life. Thus, his humanity as well as his inhumanity is delineated with consummate skill.

Moorthy, the central character in *Kanthapura* had seen a vision of the Mahatma, "mighty and god-bearing" walking between rows of volunteers (p. 32) and he stood beside the great soul. Moorthy shouted *"Gandhi Mahatma Ki Jai"* And then he listened and heard Mahatma's voice:

> There is but one force in life and that is truth, and there is but one love in life and that is the love of mankind, and there is but one God in life and that is the God of all.[7]

Moorthy has seen the Mahatma in his dream: he fell at the great leader's feet: "I am your slave", he cried. The Mahatma lifted him up and called him "my son". And then the Mahatma gave him his message of *Swadeshi* and freedom from foreign yoke. This emotional adherence of Moorthy to the Mahatma is compared with the devotional intensity of Hanuman for his God, Rama. Thus, the religious and mythological strains are brought in close association with the political thread of the novel's narratives.

A substantial part of *Kanthapura*, the novel of action and character, the novel of atmosphere and mythical lore, is concerned with portraying the political turmoil that overtakes its inhabitants and the orgy of oppression that is let loose by the police on the coolies of the Skeffington Coffee Estate of the Red-man. The story of the people's resistance against foreign rule and the police repression in Kanthapura and its adjoining areas is narrated with passion and intensity by Raja Rao from chapter 14 onwards till chapter 19—to the end of the novel.

In chapter 13, Moorthy is described as a leader exhorting the people: "Prepare yourselves for action" (p. 119). This action of the people of Kanthapura is a kind of a follow-up of the pilgrimage of the Mahatma with 82 followers to begin with. The Khadi-clad volunteers arrive in buses from distant places and join the force of non-violent non-cooperators. Range Gowda, the patel joins their ranks and the people under Moorthy's instigation refuse to pay revenue to the foreign government. They also launch a powerful campaign for prohibition, for picketing the toddy shops. Pariah Rachanna rushes to climb a toddy tree and the police beat him on his legs. The police attack the volunteers with lathis and batons, but their spirit is high as they are inspired by the Mahatma's ideals. The villagers shout with heroic enthusiasm *Mahatma Gandhi ki jai* (p. 130) and they are arrested and taken away in trucks and left unceremoniously in the midst of a thick jungle. But their spirit is irrepressible and they form a line, sing, shout, and assert their freedom and their right to fight against injustice.

Chapter 15 narrates graphically the story of repression at the Skeffington Coffee Estate, the police *zoolum* on the unarmed, innocent, poor coolies, and Moorthy's heroic resistance against this onslaught. Moorthy moves on to the bridge, looks towards the Skeffington Estate Gate and says to his companions, "March forward". His followers march on and squat down before the toddy booth (p. 137). There is a shower of rain followed by a shower of lathis directed against the poor coolies. The police beat Moorthy's men and the coolies too, who cry and scream due to pain and injuries. The police-inspector whips the coolies and Rangamma and Ratna try to resist their onslaught. Moorthy shouts passionately *Vande Mataram* and *Mahatma Gandhi ki jai* and then a blow shuts his mouth and his friends Seetharam and Nanjamma shout: "He's fallen, Moorthy. He's dead, Moorthy. Oh, you butchers!" (p.139) Moorthy is not arrested whereas Seenu, Vasudev, Subbu and Range Gowda are taken to prison. More coolies arrive in Kanthapura to swell the ranks of Gandhian non-cooperators and volunteers and the resistance seems to be growing for a while: "The army of the Mahatma is an increasing garland" (p. 140).

The movement, especially picketing of toddy shops, grows from strength to strength. Villagers from neighbouring villages, Ramput and Siddapur, join and strengthen the Gandhian non-violent army, and they launch a no-tax campaign. However, in chapter 17, Raja Rao graphically narrates the humiliation to which the coolies of the Skeffington Coffee Estate are subjected—they are made to march 'bend-headed' through the streets to publicly demonstrate their slavery and servitude. While they march blinking in the streets "even the voice of God seemed to have died out of their tongues." The police let loose a reign of terror and Rachanna, Seethamma and other women become victims of the *zoolum*. The villagers, especially women, try to seek shelter in the temple compound, but in vain. Moorthy has been arrested and Ratna takes his place as the chief of the resistance movement. The men and women perform *Satyanarayana puja* and shout "Congress, Congress and the Mahatma". Ratna blows the conch and the followers shout with zeal, *Vande Mataram* and *Inquilab Zindabad*. They sing patriotic songs and the coolies of the Estate join their ranks.

The crowd of resisters swells and then the police shower bullets on the people. The bullets "scream through the air" like "flying snakes taken fire..." and Vedamma is hurt in her leg. Some one opened the gas cylinders of the city lights and this was a signal for a massive attack. Men are kicked and beaten up and many fall victims to the bullets. More police men arrive from Maddur and intensify the repression on the people. Moorthy is in jail and the police burn and destroy houses in Kanthapura. Roofs and ceilings of houses are pulled down in the *melee* and Kanthapura, once a village of prosperity, wears the look of desolation and destruction. Kanthapura, its various quarters, its ponds, its streets—all lie in ruins. People have left Kanthapura in sheer despair. Of all the people Range Gowda alone went back to that deserted village for personal and family reasons. The people from Bombay arrive, buy land and build houses but the original Kanthapurians have been displaced and have left for other places for survival. Range Gowda describes the desolate scene of Kanthapura which is pathetic. He says:

> I drank three handfuls of Himavathy water and I said, 'Protect us, mother!' to Kenchamma and I said, 'Protect us, father' to the Siva of the promontory and I spat three times to the West and three times to the South, and I threw a palmful of dust at the sunken wretch, and I turned away. But to tell you the truth, mother, my heart it beat like a drum. [8]

This brief summation of the sequence of events in *Kanthapura* has implicit in it reflections on theme and characterisation, content and form, technique and vision—reflections which can be expanded substantially. The basic question ought to be raised: Is *Kanthapura* a unique work of art and life, a novel of unique qualities? The answer is 'yes' and 'no' depending upon what is intended and implied in the question itself.

It seems that *Kanthapura* is a unique novel of the time (1938) partly due to its highly innovative form and technique. Its form is unique because it is predominantly organic and natural—the characters, the events, the crisis, the glories of the Gandhian struggle and the desolation of the deserted village—the point where the novel ends—all seem to rise naturally in the Indian air from the soil just as wild flowers grow on a river bank. This organic quality of growth is one of the special features of *Kanthapura* as a novel, as a work of art. Moorthy, Range Gowda, Bhatta, Ratna, Subha Chetty, Rangamma, Venkamma and many other men and women seem to be rising from the soil of Kanthapura so naturally that they breathe life and activity into it and use words as natural tools of their feelings and innate desires.

Even Bhatta, the self-seeking, greedy, anti-Gandhian character has been portrayed with sympathy and a touch of humanity as well as stark realism. He voices his criticism of Gandhian ways in a manner which echoes the feelings of many others as well. He speaks of the widespread practice of dowry to Rangamma:

> It is so difficult to find bridegrooms these days. When I was in town the other day, I went to see old Subrama Pandita. And he was telling me how he could find no one for his last grand-daughter. No one. Every fellow with a Matric or an Inter asks, "What dowry do you

offer? How far will you finance my studies? I want to have this degree and that degree." Degrees. Degrees. Nothing but degrees or this Gandhi vagabondage. When there are boys like Moorthy, who should get safely married and settle down, they begin this Gandhi business. What is this Ganghi business? Nothing but weaving coarse hand-made cloth, not fit for a mop, and bellowing out bhajans and bhajans, and mixing with the Pariahs. Pariahs now come to the temple door and tomorrow they would like to be in the heart of it. They will one day put themselves in the place of the Brahmins and begin to teach the Vedas. I heard only the other day that in the Mysore Sanskrit College some Pariahs sought admission. Why, our Beadle Timmayya will come one of these days to ask my daughter in marriage! Why shouldn't he?[9]

Thus, the anti-Gandhian stance of Bhatta is pervasively portrayed and in the process he emerges as a character in his own right. He is certainly not a foil to Moorthy (as a few critics seem to believe) and though he has serious failings, he still seems to have grown organically.

Organicism, as a principle of growth, seems to be one of the most significant characteristics of *Kanthapura* as a novel, as a gallery of portraits—full, half, quarter,— living, breathing, sniffing, spitting and shouting. They all come to life through their gestures, their words, their mannerisms. Seetharama, a Brahmin in Kanthapura, "speaks of this and that . . ." and then suddenly he turns to Bhatta and says "I want your help *Bhattare*—" And Bhatta says "What can I do for you, Seetharamu? Anything you like. . ."

The form of address, *Bhaṭṭare* from Bhatta, derived from original Kannada, is indeed a meaningful expression in English since it catches the original rhythm of Kannada speech. In fact, many of Raja Rao's stylistic devices in *Kanthapura* are so effective because they carry with them the smell and the fragrance of original Kannada rhythms. *Kanthapura*'s technique of narration, derived from the *Purana* or the Puranic tale, has been much commented upon not only by his critics, but even by Raja Rao himself, and therefore repetitive references or restatement of these critical comments are better avoided.

Meaning, in *Kanthapura*, emerges from the relationship between two worlds: the fictional world created by Raja Rao out of his experience and the 'real' world, the apprehendible universe. Our understanding of *Kanthapura* will depend upon our realisation of this relationship between these two worlds. *Kanthapura* is a spectrum coloured by three hues—the social, political and mythological. *Kanthapura* is, in a sense, a novel of realistic situations, of political resurgence, a work of realism in fiction. And yet, it is not purely realistic or naturalistic. This is combined with the strains of myth, of gods and goddesses, of blind superstitious beliefs and uncanny insights. It is the image of real life, observed in a visionary state of mind. The complexities of its form arise out of this odd combination of apparently disparate state of mind which lie concealed behind its creation.

What about a 'value judgement' or the 'sense of an

Kanthapura

ending' in respect of *Kanthapura*? Our value judgement will depend upon what we make of Gandhism or Gandhian impact on our society before and after independence. Gandhian ideas are being subjected to a gruelling reassessment at present. Critics who are hostile to Gandhi and the Gandhian age may, perhaps, dub *Kanthapura* as a novel of great irresponsibility, in the *Leavisian* sense. To me, *Kanthapura* is an excellent piece of fiction because it catches a few significant moments of history in contemporary India and gives them a sense of immortality which is characteristic of great fiction. It surely is not as great a work as *The Serpent and the Rope* in range and scope. It is slender, but its tidy slenderness has an organic quality about it which will ensure for it an abiding place in modern Indo-Anglian fiction.

Notes

1. *Kanthapura* by Raja Rao. A New Directions Paperback (New York 1967) p. VII. All subsequent references are to this edition.
2. Ahmed Ali, "Illusion and Reality: The Art and Philosophy of Raja Rao" *"The Journal of Commonwealth Literature.* London, July, 1968, No. 5, p. 77.
3. M.K. Naik, *Raja Rao* (New York, 1972) p. 77.
4. Ahmed Ali, p. 17.
5. *Kanthapura*, p. 2.
6. *Ibid.*, p. 9.
7. *Ibid.*, p. 33.
8. *Ibid.*, p. 182.
9. *Ibid.*, p. 26.

AHMED ALI: *Twilight in Delhi*

Harish Trivedi

In March 1939, Ahmed Ali (b. 1910) had just completed his first novel, *Twilight in Delhi*.[1] He had written it in English, and four months later, he did the big brave thing by setting off for London with the manuscript under his arm and a letter of introduction in his pocket to that patron-saint of all aspiring Indian writers in English of those times, E.M. Forster. The voyage might have seemed to Ahmed Ali a natural enough step in a time-honoured pursuit, but it wasn't as if everything in his life upto this point had inevitably led to this grand endeavour to set the Thames on fire.

While Ahmed Ali's father had been an English-educated civil servant in the Punjab, his ancestors had for generations served as *ulema* of whom some had even officiated as the *imams* of the Jama Masjid in Delhi. Both these disparate cultural streams that Ahmed Ali inherited were to play their respective parts in his upbringing and to co-mingle in his literary sensibility. At the age of five, living in his grandmother's house in Delhi where he had been born, Ahmed Ali was sent to a *maqtab* to begin his education in the traditional manner by learning to recite the *Koran;* just how deep this seed was planted is demonstrated by its late efflorescence in an English translation of the holy book completed by Ahmed Ali in 1980. As a boy, traditionally enough again, Ahmed Ali began composing verses in Urdu, whereupon he was 'soundly discouraged'[2] and told to concentrate on learning English instead. Under the influence of two inspiring teachers, Eric C. Dickinson at Aligarh and Laurence Brander at Lucknow, Ahmed Ali then went on to take his M.A. in English at Lucknow in 1931, in a performance which won him a gold medal and a lecturership at the University.

In the meanwhile, he had been writing plays and short stories in English as well as Urdu. He was one of a group of four contributors to *Angarey* (1932), a collection of ten short stories which, more due to its *success du scandale* through proscription than any intrinsic radical fervour, is now regarded as the work that launched the Progressive Movement in Urdu Literature. Never quite easy within this Progressive avant garde led by his friend Sajjad Zaheer, Ahmed Ali finally broke away in 1938. In the meanwhile, he had published a collection of twelve Urdu short stories all his own, *Sholay* (1936), and the following year, his English translation of one of his most successful Urdu stories "Hamari Gali" was published in John Lehmann's *New Writing in English* under the title "Our Lane". Sensing that he had here hit upon the material for his magnum opus, Ahmed Ali now settled down to develop this story

Twilight in Delhi

into his first novel and, against the run of most of the fiction he had so far produced, wrote it in English.

Twilight in Delhi, published in London in 1940, did prove to be all that Ahmed Ali might have hoped it would be. One indication of just how intense and apt an imaginative investment he had made into this novel is the fact that it was not until twenty-six years later that Ahmed Ali came out with another nove, *Ocean of Night*. But this latter-day, psychological account of a good-hearted courtesan of Lucknow and her widely contrasted lovers (in broad continuation of a whole tradition of Urdu novels with the same theme and locale which had been inaugurated by Mirza Hadi 'Ruswa' in *Umrao Jan Ada,* 1900) came so long after *Twilight* and proved so inevitably disappointing and sparse in comparison that it might as well have been written by another person. To most of his admirers, Ahmed Ali remains a one-novel novelist.[3]

I

Twilight in Delhi is the story of Mir Nihal, already an old man of sixty-two when the novel opens, and of his populously ramified family and his crowded but intimately familiar neighbourhood in a by-lane of Kucha Pandit in the heart of the old walled city of Delhi ceremoniously founded on 12 May 1638 at the height of Mughul magnificence by the fifth emperor Shah Jehan and initially known after him as Shahjehanabad.[4] When the novel opens in the summer of 1911, this seat of imperial glory has already been in disgrace and decline for over a half a century, since 1857. As a consequence of the Mutiny, the last Mughal King Bahadur Shah Zafar was deposed, the fine buildings immediately around the Red Fort were razed to the ground, the great Jama Masjid was threatened with demolition and was in fact closed to all worshippers for five years as was the Fatehpuri Mosque for a full twenty, and a substantial number of the Muslim inhabitants of the city were massacred in reprisal while all the rest were driven out of the city walls, to be gradually allowed to trickle back under strict British surveillance. Mir Nihal was ten years old then, and the strategically placed flash-back in which he recalls some of these events is the structural and emotional centre of the novel. But now, in 1911, worse is to follow. A "new and foreign king . . .", "Jaraj"[5] (i.e., George V) is to be taken out in a Coronation procession from the hallowed Red Fort and, more galling still, a new imperial Delhi is to be built beyond the city walls, so that the old Mughal Delhi will eventually be seen not only to have been further rejected and bypassed but humbled forever after in comparison with its ironically juxtaposed neighbour. The fall is now complete; the sun has set on the seventh of the historical Delhis.

Twilight depicts the Coronation of 1911 and its distressing consequences through the rest of the decade for Mir Nihal as well as for Delhi in a narrative divided into four neatly structured parts. In the first part, beginning in May

1911, Delhi is viewed in a poetic-historical long shot, rather in the manner of the opening sequences of some Wessex novels by Thomas Hardy, until the camera zooms in to settle on "a net of by-lanes" (4) in the heart of the city and then on a cul-de-sac house there, the home of Mir Nihal. The bustling scene is vividly set, and the preparations described for the Coronation as well as for the coincident wedding of Mir Nihal's youngest son Asghar. In the second part, the incident of Mir Nihal the pigeon-fancier who goes out to buy some select *shirazi* pigeons to add to his depleted stock, which are then promptly eaten up by a cat is described in such loaded terms as to suggest that by it no less than the stealthy and crafty English are meant; Mir Nihal's old love the courtesan Babban Jan dies, to deal him a double blow; and, finally on 7 December, the Coronation takes place which Mir Nihal with all the others goes to look at but hardly sees as his mind wanders back to 1857. In the third part, the first two chapters describe Asghar's wedding as the last two chapters of Part II had described the Coronation; these parallel events together constitute the climax of the novel. Hardly have the guests departed when the inordinately romantic Asghar grows disillusioned in his lovely but placid wife Bilqeece; Mir Nihal's daughter Mehro is given away in what proves to be another unhappy marriage; a couple of years pass, and Mir Nihal is one day suddenly brought down by an obviously symbolic paralytic stroke. In the meanwhile, the construction of New Delhi and the despoilation of old Delhi have grown apace; a bomb has been thrown at Lord Hardinge; and the War, here seen as another alien agent of disruption, has begun. In the last part, as the decade comes to a close, a post-War influenza epidemic kills thousands in the city; the miserably neglected Bilqeece dies; all too suddenly, Mir Nihal's dearest son Habibuddin also dies a kind of vicarious death while Mir Nihal himself lingers on through these multiplying deaths and through "the death of the world in which he had been born" (275), himself "more dead than alive" (287) but not yet afforded the final release as the novel ends. Beyond the four walls to which he is now confined, the Rowlatt Bill has been passed and the British have on 30 March 1919 fired into a protesting crowd in Chandni Chowk, killing the son of a shopkeeper from Mir Nihal's own lane, but the great wave of national struggle that now arises remains only a dim and distant presence in this novel. Its moribund gloom and crepuscular ambience allow no room for any glimmer of hope for the future.

However, this outline of the major events is not only necessarily inadequate but, in the case of this novel, also a vital distortion. Any suggestion of a coherent plot here, or any conscious literary plan to which it might have been written, is utterly overwhelmed by the almost autonomously rich texture; by the all-subsuming 'feel' of it. The events in this novel are not organically related; they are not in any way anticipated or prepared for with the exception of the two climactic celebrations; and, most importantly, they do not arise one from the other to form any kind of a flow. The most successful of the scenes and episodes are all detachable set-pieces; the kite-flying that fills the sky (27-29), the dust-storm (62-65), the visit by Asghar and Bari to the courtesan Mushtari Bai (73-74), the splendidly evoked Friday market on the steps of the Jama Masjid where Mir Nihal buys his pigeons among a connoisseurs' discussion of the relative merits of the *shirazi, kabuli, nisavray* and *golay* breeds of the bird (99-106), the Ramazan and Eed (129-37), the marvellous wedding, surely worthy to rank among the most elaborate and joyous weddings in all fiction (159-85), and Habibuddin's terminal illness, during which every visitor "brought a new cure" (276-81). Even to call this novel episodic may be to impose on it a literary pattern such as it neither possesses nor aims at, for it is atleast quite as scenic as it is episodic.

Besides, not only can the sequence of most of the events in this novel be easily shuffled but the total time-scheme within which they are set seems collapsible as well. The depredation of the old city between 1911 and 1919 is inexorable without being continuous or cumulative, while the personal and domestic events seem to be located virtually outside the time-axis. As he proceeds from the age of sixty-two to seventy-one, Mir Nihal is not seen to grow older or sadder or anything, nor is there any perceptible change wrought within any of the other characters by the succession of events or the march of time. *Twilight* may, in a few of its more self-conscious passages, be a meditation on Time, but of time passing as felt on the pulse of its characters it offers little evidence.

II

Nor are *Twilight's* characters really characters. Not only do they not grow or change, they hardly have an inside to them. Mir Nihal is not seized of any of the sentiments he expresses; he is merely an appropriately conceived vehicle for them. His youngest son Asghar, whom his father distantly disapproves of for his new 'farangi' ways, is more vacuous than rebellious or maudlin; there simply isn't enough to him of the human stuff. His father and he, relatively the two most prominent and contrasted characters in the novel, hardly spend any time together or even speak to each other, a fact widely representative of the lack of any real interaction or engagement between any two characters in the novel. Each character is throughout the same and sufficient unto himself, and his appearances in the novel are so many reproductions of the same vignette.

To consider all this as a failing on the part of Ahmed Ali would, however, be utterly to misread the novel. Ahmed Ali has no characters in the recognized sense because they would not be to his artistic purpose; it is not a human being but the city, the city as a human conglomerate, that is his hero. All his numerous characters are quickly and strongly realized in visual terms, and yet they

Twilight in Delhi

do not even form a portrait gallery. Rather, they are seen by us as the figures in one of those vibrantly crowded Breughel paintings in which literally hundreds of human beings fill one frame, all enclosed in a living common space all bound together by a palpable sense of community. *Twilight* has close to ninety characters jostling within its 288 pages, and they feel like half as many more because by the time a Saeed Hasan or a Nazrul Hasan reappears on page 182 or 279 after having been briefly introduced on page 58 or page 183, we have very likely forgotten who he is.

Indeed, the one device of systematic individuation that Ahmed Ali adopts is not only delectably apt in the context but serves at the same time further to strengthen the sense of commonality; the characters are to be known and remembered by their beards. There are atleast twenty-five distinctly described beards in the novel, including some adorning anonymous faces; the barber's "black curly beard" (22), the "long beard" of "an oldish man in the crowd" which "fell over his chest in a fine array' (23), Ghafoor's "black beard, oval in shape, with the hair on the cheekbones shaved off" (37), Nisar Ahmad's "expensive fan-shaped beard...dyed red with henna" (92), Sheikh Mohammad Sadiq's beard, "conical and small" (93), the mad faqir Mast Qalandar's "matted beard, full of dust and soup and dirt, ... tousled, looking like a bulbul's nest." (95), Khwaja Asraf Ali's beard, "close-cropped on the cheeks, (which) terminated in a slightly pointed end of half-black and half-grey hair" (101), the poet Nawab

Sirajuddin Khan Saeel's "Impressive flowing beard" (117), the mystical faqir Kamaal Shah's "long, shaggy beard" (125), Ahmad Wazir the family barber's "sparse yet longish beard" (162), the venerable and pious Mir Ejaz Hussain's "very long beard" which goes "all awry" as it is subjected to boisterous indignity during Asghar's high spirited wedding (164, 165), on which occasion Sharfullah's beard also gets "besmeared in the foul-smelling oil" in a practical joke (181), Meraj's "black bushy beard" to go with his "ferocious eyes of a madman" (194), Mirza the milk-seller's "conical white beard (which) seemed to be pointed and sharp like a dagger" and aptly so, as he launches into the most impassioned diatribe in the whole novel against the "illegally begotten ones, these Farangis" (219-20), the witch-doctor Moulvi Saheb's "black oval beard, (with) long curly hair reaching down to his waist" (280), and finally, Mir Nihal's "white and well-combed beard. . . parted in the middle", which gave "his noble face a majestic look" as we first see him, which later in the novel is pecked at by his dying pigeons in "so loving and tender an action", in which "white and majestic beard" he looks "magnificent" at Eed, which he strokes with pleasure when he approves of a dish cooked by Bilqeece, which has gone "all awry" as he lies in bed after his paralytic stroke, and which is finally "unkempt and dirty" as he mourns the death of his favourite son (7, 112, 133, 223, 286).

"Now everyone from all classes wears beards,"[6] the poet Ghalib had fastidiously complained of the unsettled post-Mutiny society in Delhi in 1859; from Ahmed Ali we may know that they indeed did, even half a century later. To crown it all, there is yet another faqir in the novel who is known simply as "Red Beard" (122) and, shortly before he dies, the pious Habibuddin dreams (in the kind of surealistic sequence which is rare enough here but occurs more frequently and persuasively in Ahmed Ali's more 'modern' second novel *Ocean of Night*) that walking alone on a vast plain he meets a man with a red beard who asks Habibuddin to follow him but, presently, "as I looked, his beard vanished and red flames appeared all around, and the plain caught fire" (277).

III

Twilight then has, instead of an organic plot, discrete scenes and events strung loosely along the slender thread of clock-time, and, instead of realized individual characters, a whole sea of humanity, a city full of people most of whom are recognized and remembered by us by some trick of persona such as a hirsute emblem on their chins, and who discontinuously flit in and out of distant corners of the novel as out of far-flung booths at a fair-ground. *Twilight* is thus neither a novel of action or plot, nor a novel of character or manners. It is, rather, a novel of a historical moment, a novel of a community, and above all else, a novel of place. *Twilight* creates, celebrates, laments and immortalizes a vitally human place as few novels have ever been able to do, and therein lies its quintessential distinction.

This place, of course, is the Lal Kuan Bazar part of old Delhi, which extends from Hauz Qazi through Bazar Sirkiwalan past Lal Darwaza to the Fatehpuri Mosque at the bottom of Chandni Chowk. Off this road to the left is Kuncha Pandit and within it, in Jangli Kuan, in Mohalla Niyariyan, lives Mir Nihal. Just as it is not Mir Nihal or any other single character on whom this novel focuses but rather on the community which they together constitute, so what is described most vividly in it is not the particular house Mir Nihal lives in but the neighbourhood that 'places', and surrounds it. The complex web of lanes and by-lanes is given its precise topographical context; the different approaches to Kucha Pandit are set down in detail as characters walk back to it on various occasions from various parts of the city: Asghar from Mushtari Bai's *Kotha* in Chaori Bazar via Hauz Qazi and Lal Darwaza, for example (79), or Mir Nihal from the shop in Chandni Chowk via the Clock Tower and Balli Maran (90-91). But the most significant of the descriptions is the very first one, right at the beginning of the novel:

> a net of alleys goes deep into the bowels of the city shooting from Lala Kuan, and going into Kucha Pandit turns to the right and terminates at Mohalla Niyariyan, which has a net of by-lanes of its own. One branch of it comes straight on, tortuous and winding, growing narrower like the road of life, and terminates at the

house of Mir Nihal. As you look at it only a wall faces you, and in that wall a door. Nothing else (4-5)

The narrowing of the road of life until it comes up at the bottom of a cul-de-sac against a wall— 'nothing else' —is obviously, and perhaps all too heavily, symbolic of the terminal stage of the way of life here being depicted, but for the rest of the novel we are given the rich human fullness of this life, without much impedence from ominous symbol or metaphor, which makes its passing away a matter of poignant regret. These lanes and by-lanes are constantly overflowing with life rather than daunted by a terminal blankness. The earth is ever thick with shop-keepers and vendors and faqirs and beggars and all kinds of people ambling to and fro at all hours of the day and night, and the very sky is full of flocks of trained pigeons trying to outsoar each other and of colourful kites being skilfully flown:

> The sky was full of kites, black kites and white kites, purple kites and blue. They were green and lemon coloured, red and peacock blue and yellow, jade and vermilion, plain or of various patterns and in different colours, black against yellow, red against white, mauve alternating with green, pink with purple, striped or triangular, with moons on them or stars and wings and circles in different colours, forming such lovely and fantastic designs. There were small kites and big kites, (kites) flying low and kites that looked studded in the

sky. They danced and they capered, they dipped down or rose erect with the elegance of cobras. They whirled and wheeled and circled, chased each other or stood static in mid air. There was a riot of kites in the sky (28).

As with the kites so with other things and even people in *Twilight*. There is an infinite variety, a veritable riot, of them in the novel. Nor do most of them seem to mean much beyond what meets the eye; they just plenteously and joyously *are*.

And much of what is seen is also heard. The lanes resound with the cries of vocal and witty vendors or with the choric comments of groups of women or artisans or with their impassioned arguments or with the sound 'from all around' of qawwalis being sung late at night or simply with the constant hum of life. This overflow of quotidian sound is transcended periodically by a sound yet more compelling in its message, the *azaan* or the call to prayer sung out from the minaret-top by a particularly inspired exponent of the art, Nisar Ahmad the ghee-seller:

> Just as the sun had set his golden voice would rise gradually in the air and, rippling with the glory of Islam, would unfold its message to the Mussalmans, bringing with it a sense of the impermanence of life and the transience of the world. His voice could be heard far and wide in several mohallas, rising above the din and noise of the town, leaping to the stars. Then

slowly it would come to an end, bringing with it peace and silence, acting as a lullaby to the tired hearts of men (92-93; also heard elsewhere on 30, 87, 97, 128, 223 and 252).

The rich sensory vibrancy of this little world and its exuberant vitality depend for their existence on an implicit sense of perfect communal integrity and of security by enclosure, just as its superb sense of confidence and self-sufficiency derive from its past imperial glory. And if this world feels itself to be under a dire and fatal threat during the decade depicted in the novel, it is because this integrity and security and confidence are now being increasingly encroached upon from without and undermined from within. The foreign ruler ensconced in distant Calcutta is beyond the ken of Mir Nihal and his neighbours, but the sight of King George V setting out in imperial progress from their very own Red Fort causes them unbearable humiliation and anguish. Within the house, Mir Nihal is indignant with Asghar for wearing English pumps: "I will have no aping of the Farangis in my house. Throw them away." (11). Later, when Asghar gives a pair of English shoes to his wife Bilqeece to wear, the ladies in the *zenana* are as outraged and even more outspoken: "She looks like as good-as-dead Farangans" one says, and another that she seems "to have eaten some Farangi's shit" (195). But Mir Nihal's is a lost cause: "that unity of experience and form, which existed in Mir Nihal's youth, had vanished. . . a new world had come into being and, he felt, he was not part of it." (251). Towards the end of the novel, as he lies dying, he sees the new order triumphing, and does not even protest any more: "Asghar often came now wearing English clothes, but his father did not say anything." (252).

Beyond the home, there are any number of other similar changes to lament. In the streets can now be heard incredibly cheap verses sung in vulgar tunes, and they make Mir Nihal reflect:

> What had happened to the great poets of Hindustan? Where were Mir and Ghalib and Insha? Where were Dard and Sauda or even Zauq? . . . Time had reversed the order of things, and life had been replaced by a death-in-life. No beauty seemed to remain anywhere and ugliness had blackened the face of Hindustan . . . (252).

Even the language of ordinary conversation has been debased, and the whole "culture and its purity. . . its chastity and form" (3) are in grave peril.

In more concrete terms, not only is a new Delhi coming up to dwarf and relegate this one but some of the best loved features and landmarks within Delhi are being obliterated as well. "The stalwart trees that stood in rows in the middle of the bazar from Fatehpuri to the Fountain and beyond," the "noble and expansive peepal tree," that ran down the middle of Chandni Chowk and had for generations provided shade and shelter, are finally hacked down and the "uniqueness and oriental atmosphere" of this proud bazar destroyed (90, 138, 205).

> This affected the people more deeply than anything else. For this was the bazar through which they had walked day in and day out throughout their lives. With these changes it looked quite new, not the real Chandni Chowk with which so many memories were associated (205).[7]

The final and ultimate outrage, however, is that "The city walls were also going to be demolished (205). When they are, it is as if the city has been denuded, its integrity and very virtue violated, and a breach made through which all the forces of degradation and destruction are let in. In the summer of 1918, the loo bearing sand from the outlying deserts

> howled more fiercely than before as the City Walls had been demolished and the wind could now blow free from the mountainous wastes outside the city. It howled through the empty streets and in the narrow by-lanes and bazars. The dogs moaned and wept at night as if afraid of death and the cats. . . were quiet and subdued (242).

IV

So comprehensively successful is Ahmed Ali in evoking the city in *Twilight* that there is a little danger of our taking his success entirely for granted, of mistaking the Delhi of his artistic creation for the actual Delhi that has existed and, notwithstanding the momentous alterations described above, still continues to exist. It may be useful, therefore, to note that though Ahmed Ali had known Kucha Pandit well as a child and had in fact been born in the house which served him as a model for Mir Nihal's, he had grown up and later lived and worked elsewhere, in Azamgarh, Aligarh and Lucknow. When he decided in the summer of 1938 to work "Hamari Gali" into this novel, he felt the need to make a conscientious field-trip to his roots, as he has recounted to Carlo Coppola in an interview:

> I had the idea in (*sic*) the back of my mind that I wanted to write this novel. I went and met as many people as I could and I watched everyone's actions as I walked down the street. I watched everything. . . I went to the Jama Masjid. I watched everyone—the pigeon sellers, the pigeon-buyers, the pigeon-flyers—all those wonderful kaleidoscopic scenes and crowds. I also looked from the steps of the Jama Masjid at the Red Fort in the distance. . . I kept on watching, observing and imagining. I would try to see as many people in the *Mohalla* as possible, as many members of my family as I could. . . I went to see everyone. I was glad that it pleased my mother, but she did't know I was doing it with something else in the back of my mind.[8]

Five years after the publication of *Twilight* in London, E.M. Forster, who had offered crucial help in its publication, revisited India, stayed in Delhi with his 'beloved Ahmed' and was taken round by him not only to the famous historical monuments but to his private literary sanctorum as well. On 2 November 1945, they spent the day at Tughlaqabad—Adilabad, and in the evening, as Ahmed Ali narrates, he took Forster on a walk:

> Straight from the back of the Jama Masjid down the colourful Chaori Bazar and via Hauz Qazi and Lal Kuan. . . to Kucha Pandit. . . whose by-lanes. . . got narrower and narrower at every turn until they terminated at my ancestral home. . . consisting of two houses, one built by my paternal grandfather after the "Mutiny," the other by my maternal grandfather, interlinked through doors opening into a vestibule.'

In the 1966 'Introduction' to the first Indian reprint of *Twilight* written from the aggravating, nostalgic distance of Karachi, Ahmed Ali said that what the government of independent India had done to old Delhi was far worse than what the British had (vii). It is true that, in 1985, at the corner of the entrance to Kucha Pandit off the Lal Kuan Bazar (now officially, but only officially, called 'Hamdard Marg'), there stands the 'Go-go Tea House and Property Dealers,' that a cinema-house called Excelsior lies within shouting distance from Kucha Pandit on the way to Hauz Qazi (but this looks old enough to have existed in Ahmed Ali's time if not in Mir Nihal's), and that in the labyrinthine depths of Kucha Pandit, at the entrance to Gali Jangli Kuan where the lane is no wider than six feet, there has sprung up a tailor's shop specializing in "Jean Codowray (i.e., Corduroy Jeans) and Gents Variety", the kind of Farangi sartorial intrusion that would make Mir Nihal turn in his grave. But there are any number of little shops in the neighbourhood still stacked from floor to ceiling with all kinds of kites, flocks of pigeons still flutter off from high perches periodically to speckle the sky, and the *azaan* from numerous mosques still punctuates the street sounds though now amplified through multi-directional loudspeakers.

V

Because it evokes so well a dying culture and an engulfed city and the sense of their transience, it has been a critical commonplace to acclaim *Twilight,* as, above all, a poetic novel, indeed a lyrical novel. Anita S. Kumar, for example, has classed Ahmed Ali as a lyrical novelist with "Herman Hesse, Virginia Woolf, Andre Gide, Jose Luis Borges and others," suggested that the novel possesses "a fragile sublimity . . . a piquancy and a sustained beauty not possible outside simple present tense forms" and admired "the peculiar quality of lyrical phemes" deployed in this novel. All this may well be as she puts it, but when she goes on to say that "Ahmed Ali rejects the narrative norms which are social or factual," that "the emphasis is not on events and circumstances leading up to the events, it is on words which are phonological, metonymic and meitoc (i.e., meoitic)," and then concludes that "The ethical potentiality of the sentences is reduced to a metonymic attribute of phomene (i.e., phoneme)[10]," some problems arise beyond those of comprehending precisely what she might mean.

The question here surely is whether, even if the above descriptions of the phemes, phonemes and tenses used by Ahmed Ali are coherent and apt, they lead us any nearer the source of his power to move us. It may be argued that while such palpable linguistic and stylistic devices may generate a sense of obvious poeticality, they do not make for true poetry. Nor do such insistent overtures by Ahmed Ali himself to symbolism as the cats and the pigeons and the dust-storm, which Anita S. Kumar makes much of, or the palm tree and the henna tree standing in Mir Nihal's courtyard, which are both heavily redolent of pristine Islam and are both worked over-time in a particularly pathetic fallacy as their leaves "sere" and fall off (7, 12, 19, 42, 80, 83, 98, 114-116, 193, 226, 266, 279 and inevitably at the end, 287-88). Overriding all such overt gestures and in fact redeeming the novel from them, there is also in *Twilight* a far more substantial proportion of something else of that "solidity of specification" and "value by saturation," which Ahmed Ali here achieves in ways more direct and unpremeditated than Henry James' fine and elaborate mind could have conceived of. In the event, it is the fully realized richness of its social and historical fabric that makes for the poignance of its passing away and not any normative stylistic devices. The tenses of verbs and the phemes and the phonemes may contribute a facile lyrical effect but the poetry of *Twilight* (as was remarked on another occasion) lies in the city.

VI

But a larger and more vital corrective to the common view of *Twilight in Delhi* as a poem in prose or an exquisite reverie would be to insist outright that it is no less a political novel than a poetic one, in its profound and integral engagement with the forces of society and history and communal and national destiny. It needs to be reiterated that at the centre of this novel Ahmed Ali has placed the most majestic political spectacle that the British ever mounted in India, the Coronation Durbar of George V, the only British sovereign ever to set foot in his predominant colony. In pointed juxtaposition, Ahmed Ali then frames this event historically by describing, immediately preceeding the Coronation, a visit to the *Zenana* of Mir Nihal's house by Gul Bano, ' a grand-daughter of Bahadur Shah' the last Mughal empeor, who even proceeds to sing one of her father's poems of political lament (142-44), and by contriving, immediately after the imperial procession has passed, to have Mir Nihal run into Mirza Nasirul Mulk 'the youngest son of Bahadur Shah' who is now reduced to abject beggary (155-56). Some days before the royal event, the women in Mir Nihal's house have berated 'these beaten-with-the-broom Farangis,' 'these good-as dead Farangis' and compared them adversely with the magnificent Mughals (139), and the day before the Coronation, Mir Nihal with his son Habibuddin and the Faqir Kambal Shah sits discussing 'the causes of the downfall of the Mughals', not academically as they are still discussed in all the history class-rooms of India, but as a fact of continuing vital importance to themselves (145-46).

On the day itself, while watching the Royal procession, Mir Nihal's blood-shot eyes unfocus to dwell in a long flash-back on the atrocities that the British had perpetrated against the people of Delhi in 1857 and the glorious suicidal battle that some Muslims had then waged against Sir Thomas Metcalfe to ensure the survival of the Jama Masjid (150-52). As he reflects.

> There were those men of 1857 and here were the men of 1911, chicken-hearted and happy in their disgrace. This thought filled him with pain, and he sat there, as it were, on the rack, weeping dry tears of blood, seeing the death of his world and of his birthplace (152).

So acute is his sense of 'the sorrows of subjection' here and such the partisan emotional force of this whole flashback that when *Twilight in Delhi* was being typeset for publication by the Hogarth Press owned and managed by Leonard and Virginia Woolf, the printers struck when they came to this passage, declaring it to be 'subversive of law and order'. It was only through the influential intervention of Desmond McCarthy at E.M. Forster's instance and of Harold Nicolson, who was then the official censor at Virginia Woolf's, that the novel could be published at all.[11]

In his comprehensive survey of Nationalism in *Indo-Anglian Fiction,* Gobinda Prasad Sarma is baffled by *Twilight in Delhi* on two counts. He cannot decide whether it is a 'social novel' or a 'political' one, and even tries the category 'socio-political' to see if that would fit, and, more significantly, he eventually refuses to consider *Twilight* as a political novel "because the political nationalist spirit breathed by the novel does not belong to any recognized phase of our freedom struggle."[12] But this alleged disability turns into something of a virtue if we recall that the novel deliberately stops just when the first major 'recognized phase' of our freedom struggle begins: in fact, the incipient nationalist movement is openly repudiated by Mir Nihal:

> The Home Rule movement was started... But somehow, all this did not affect Mir Nihal. It was not for him, the martyrdom and glory in the cause of the Mother Land. His days had gone, and a new era of hopes and aspirations, which he neither understood nor sympathized with, was beginning to dawn (250).

The new hopes and aspirations are not for Mir Nihal not only because the emotional thrust of the whole novel is backward rather than forward but also because the quiddity of Mir Nihal as well as of his little world is essentially and intensely Muslim in a way that the countrywide nationalist movement could not be. In fact, such is the communal integrity of *Twilight* that not one of its numerous characters is a Hindu—except Dr. Mitra, whose name is spelt in two different ways by Ahmed Ali on the two occasions when he briefly appears, who as a trained doctor is seen as an agent of 'a foreign modernity' and brought in by the westernized black sheep of the family Asghar only when all the hakims including the legendary Hakim Ajmal Khan have failed, who predictably diagnoses the disease as tuberculosis on both occasions and fails to cure it anyhow, and who is the only character in the whole novel who is mocked at for the funny way in which he speaks (236, 278). Thoughout the novel, in fact, by Delhi is meant the Muslim Delhi founded by the Mughals, and by the people of Delhi are meant its Muslim inhabitants, through an artistic selectivity further highlighted by the historical fact that within the walled city as well as in the wider Delhi municipal area, Hindus had throughout been more numerous since before the Mutiny.[13] Elsewhere in the novel, Ahmed Ali makes a reverent nod or two towards the older history of this ancient city, as when he refers to an earlier capital founded here by 'Raja Yudhishtra in 1453 B.C.' (2) except that he has here got the spelling wrong as well as the date. And when he for once comes up with a Hindu analogy— "a gentle sadness in the heart like the music of a Yogi playing upon his sitar on some mountainside" (214)—the image he evokes is as exotically improbable as any ever dreamed up by a Californian travel-writer. But these are rare false touches, the *outre* aberrations which parodoxically serve to assure us further of the authenticity of the ambience and the experience which Ahmed Ali makes the exclusive stuff of this novel. There were, indeed, many like Mir Nihal who did honestly believe that India had always been Muslim before the British came. For example, in a memorably fervent expression of past Muslim glory in *A Passage to India* whose chronology overlaps that of *Twilight,* Aziz (equally an admirer of the great Mughals) recites during his illness a poem by Ghalib which is full of pathos, upon which all the persons assembled in the room, all Muslims, grow quiet. "Not as a call to battle, but as a calm assurance came the feeling that India was one; Moslem; always had been. . ."[14] It must have been with reference to this aspect of contemporary Muslim sensibility as much as to anything else that Forster was to acknowledge that "The civilization, or blend of civilizations, which produced Aziz has been movingly evoked by the novelist Ahmed Ali in his *Twilight in Delhi.*"[15]

VII

If it is a poem by Ghalib which triggers off a resurgence of Muslim pride in *A Passage to India,* the corresponding sentiment in *Twilight* is kept afloat by a veritable anthology of Urdu and Persian verse. A total of 265 lines of verse or song are quoted on more than fifty separate occasions in the novel, and though several of these are folk-songs such as songs of *Savan* (the monsoon) or wedding songs, and some are comic-satiric verses such as a couplet against the Rowlatt Bill (259), another against the haughty pretensions of the English and their Indian imitators (260), yet another on the malady of piles (103), and a quartrain on how Eed brings about an opportunity for disguised homosexual embrace (134), there still remains enough of classical poetry to serve the needs of ten ordinary novels. Each of the four parts of the novel carries a verse epigraph: Bahadur Shah Zafar, the emperor-poet, is copiously represented in extracts as long as twelve lines and twenty lines at a time (136, 144), Begum Nihal too can quote 'from a poet' when sufficiently roused (57), and even past ten at night a stray anonymous figure on the street can recite four lines of Persian verse and then fade out of the novel altogether (109-10).

In contrast with this capacious cultural reservoir in which the novel is aptly steeped, the few self-conscious English poetic tags employed by Ahmed Ali as the narrator make a sorry show indeed. The insistently 'insidious' by-lanes of Kucha Pandit evoke 'The Love Song of J. Alfred Prufrock' in vain (4), the Shelleyan strings of the lyre snap without any apparent local resonance (214), Keats quite gratuitously provides 'the viewless wings of the air' (13), the confusion between waking and a dream

(14), as well as the irresistible 'fever and the fret' (232), and the mad faqir who 'looked more than a Caliban, of the earth earthy' (271) seems quite hard done by the application of the Bard. To complete this woefully limited and predictable ragbag of quotable quotes, we find even the simple title-phrase of the novel embedded deep in some T.S. Eliot fustian:

> He (Mir Nihal) remained where he was, living in a constant twilight of velleities and regret... (250).

So inordinately enamoured is Ahmed Ali of this patently poetic phrase,[16] which presumably communicates before it is understood, that he trots it out again, now all but personified, towards the conclusion of his other novel *Ocean of Night* as well: "Side by side, velleities and regret appeared."[17]

In fact, the English that Ahmed Ali writes off his own bat throughout *Twilight* is no less inept and gawky. To confine ourselves to only half a dozen examples: Shams is in the habit of "closing himself up in the room with his wife" (43); "The sand had come to the centre of the sky" (62); "What! Mir Nihal said with an angry surprise" (58); "It had been heated just a little too little" (127); "But she was young and beautiful and Asghar had built most beautiful castles around her lovely frame" (187); "They persuaded him to agree, but he refused to listen to them" (194); and "There were fewer pigeons on the sky" (226). After the cumulative impact of scores of such sentences the temptation is great to say—*horrendo referens*

—that this novel could have been written only by a Professor of English who has taught in his time at such eminent institutions as the University of Lucknow, the University of Allahabad, Presidency College, Calcutta, the National Central University of China at Nanking and the University of Karachi, not to mention several assorted American universities.

But so irresistible is the artistic integrity and the imaginative truth of this novel that Ahmed Ali can hardly do anything wrong in it even if he tries. One paradoxical effect of the strange, unsettled quality of his English is that the utterly un-English world he describes is further authenticated, as not having been distorted or falsified by an incongruously superimposed alien perspective. So insistent and ubiquitous is what linguists call 'first-language interference' in this novel that, as through a glass darkly, we find ourselves constantly peering through the English in an attempt to discern behind it the inevitably Urdu original (as, for example, in nearly all the six sentences cited above). The bilingualism of much Indo-Anglian fiction is arch or prim and covert; here, it is ingenuously, even winsomely blatant. *Twilight in Delhi* is one Indo-Anglian novel screaming to be translated back into its 'original' language, like Bottom back to humanity,[18] and through an apt coincidence, it has indeed been so rendered, to the happiest of effects, by Ahmed Ali's own wife Biqees Jehan.

Ahmed Ali himself has acknowledged that many who

have read only *Dilli ki Sham* have marvelled that it could originally have been written in English.[19] But perhaps those of us who read *Twilight* in English and find it to be as compelling and authentic a novel as Ahmed Ali has made it have reason to marvel even more. For the truth seems to be that *Twilight* is a novel written not only in recognizable Urdu idiom and collocations and on occasion syntax, but also out of an Urdu sensibility and an Urdu literary tradition. The rambling disposition of scenes and episodes and the quick, colourful characterization here immediately recall Sarshar's seminal Urdu novel *Fasana-e-Azad* (1878-79) and both the theme and the tone of *Twilight* derive directly from that unique Urdu verse-form, *shehrashob,* a lament on a misgoverned, depraved or ruined city, with a glance perhaps towards Hali's *Musaddas* (1879), that immensely popular and influential lament on the decline of Islam which was acclaimed in a history of Urdu literature published in 1928 as "the greatest poem of the last 100 years."[20] Correspondingly, Fielding and Richardson have little to do with this rather un-novel like novel, and the great tradition of the English novel that they gave rise to, has left few marks on it. *Twilight in Delhi,* in consonance with its grand theme, is very likely the most indigenous and home-spun of all Indo-Anglian novels, and if it is a triumph, as it undoubtedly is, it is so in utter disregard of the alien literary language and form which are to all appearances its putative progenitors.

Notes

1. The essential facts of Ahmed Ali's life and literary career are here taken from the most substantial and well-researched account of the novelist so far, Carlo Coppola's "Ahmed Ali" (unpublished, 212 pp. ts.) I am greatly indebted to Professor Coppola as well as to Dr. Sujit Mukherjee for a preview of this illuminating work.
2. Coppola, p. 32.
3. Ahmed Ali has lately written a third novel. "Of Rats and Diplomats", which is yet to be published; it is described in Coppola, pp. 140-49.
4. For interesting accounts of the city through the nineteenth century and the early twentieth century see Akhtar Qamber (tr. and introd.) Farhatullah Baigh's *The Last Musha'irah of Delhi* (New Delhi: Orient Longman, 1979); Narayani Gupta, *Delhi Between Two Empires 1803-1931: Society, Government and Urban Growth* (Delhi: Oxford University Press, 1981); and Donald D. Ferrell, "Delhi, 1911-1922; Society and Politics in the New Imperial Capital of India" (Unpublished Ph.D. Thesis, Australian National University, Canberra, 1966).
5. *Twilight in Delhi* (London: The Hogarth Press, 1940; rpt. Bombay: Oxford University Press, 1967; rpt. paperback ed., New Delhi: Sterling Publishers Private Ltd., 1973), pp. 90,221. All subsequent quotations

from the novel, from the Sterling paperback edition, are identified within the text by page numbers in parenthesis.

6. *Khutoot-e-Ghalib* (Letters of Ghalib), p. 222; quoted by Narayani Gupta, p. 51.
7. For two photographs of Chandni Chowk with the peepal trees, see plates entitled "Improvements'; Town Hall and Clock Tower," and "Those spacious days: Chandni Chowk," in Narayani Gupta, between pp. 96 and 97.
8. Ahmed Ali, quoted in Coppola, pp. 91-92.
9. Ahmed Ali quoted in E.M. Forster; *The Hill of Devi and other Indian Writings.* ed. Elizabeth Heinz (London: Edward Arnold, 1983), p. 259.
10. Anita S. Kumar, "*Twilight in Delhi:* A Study in Lyricism," "*Indian Literature,* XIX: 2 (March-April 1976), 25-38; quotations from pp. 25-27, 35.
11. See Ahmed Ali's own account in his "Introduction" to *Twilight in Delhi,* pp. v-vi; Ahmed Ali here misspells Harold Nicolson as "Nicholson," a common enough error.
12. Gobinda Prasad Sarma, *Nationalism in Indo-Anglian Fiction* (New Delhi: Sterling Publishers, 1978), p. 130.
13. See, for example Donald D. Ferrell, p. 60, Table 1-B, which shows that there were 121, 735 Hindus to 102 952 Muslims in 1921, in the Delhi Municipal Area, while within the city, the numerical difference was

far more acute with 36,919 Hindus to 11,752 Muslims in 1921; figures for 1911 are not separately available in the *Census of India,* on which this Table is based. See also Narayani Gupta, p. 46, for a graph of "population" for the period 1845-to 1931.

14. E.M. Forster, *A Passage to India* (Penguins 1975), p. 102.
15. E.M. Forster, "Author's Notes." *A Passage to India* (London: Dent, Everyman's Library ed., 1942, rpt. 1968); p. x x x
16. T.S. Eliot wrote:"—And so the conversation slips Among velleities and carefully caught regret," "Portrait of a Lady," 11. 14-15: *Selected Poems* (London: Faber and Faber, 1963), p. 17.
17. *Ocean of Night* (London: Peter Owen, 1964; rpt. Delhi: Hind Pocket Books, 1972), p. 159.
18. Quince says to Bottom, "Bless thee, Bottom, bless thee; Thou art translated," when Bottom wakes up with an ass's head (A Midsummer Night' Dream, *III. i: 113-14);* he is translated back in IV.i. 199.
19. "Introduction", *Twilight in Delhi,* P. vii.
20. T. Grahame Bailey, *A History of Urdu Literature* Delhi; Sumit Publications, 1979), p. 4.

KAMALA MARKANDAYA: *Nectar in a Sieve*

N.K. Jain

Kamla Markandaya's *Nectar in a Sieve* (1954) is a remarkable achievement because it presents an authentic picture of village life in transition, particularly of rural poverty and hunger. As part of this picture the writer brings into sharp focus what she has herself called "the stupefying degree of endurance and resignation"[1] of which the Indian peasant is capable. The "two great and disastrous obsessions" of the Indian novel, according to K.B. Vaid, are "propaganda and sentimentality."[2] Though *Nectar* furnishes excellent material for both, the novelist's remarkable sense of restraint enables her to voice her criticism of the socio-economic system and to depict suffering without yielding either to the temptation to raise her voice or to jerk the last tear from the eyes of the readers. This paper studies the narrative technique of the novel in relation to its theme and style. And it suggests that a large part of the writer's success in the novel results from her happy choice of Rukmani not only as the central character but also as the central consciousness through which the events come filtered to the readers.

Nectar in a Sieve

Rukmani is both a participant and an observer in the novel, besides being a narrator. A peasant woman, it need hardly be said, plays a pivotal role in the household. Whatever happens in and to the family affects her directly and intimately. Rukmani is the wife of a poor tenant farmer and this fact dooms the family to a precarious existence. As such the writer's projection of her as the narrator-protagonist enables us to get a close-up of life as it is lived by such a family—its brief periods of joy, its agonizing, losing, struggle to survive, the desertion or death of sons, the experience of hunger and the extremes to which it can drive some, and the final eviction of the family from the land. Interwoven with her narrative are such aspects of Indian life as child marriage, dowry, longing for and expectations from sons, Indian hospitality and superstitious beliefs, and such intimate details as the gathering of cowdung, the pounding of chillies and the use of outstretched hand to measure cloth. The location of the village is not particularized, but all these details help to give a true feel of village life as it was lived in pre-Independence India. As an expatriate with Western affluence in her mind, Markandaya's picture of Indian poverty tends to be overdrawn, but the presentation is still relevant because it is substantially correct even today. A first hand first person account of the happenings not only lends greater authenticity to the picture but also enables the writer to achieve effects of depth and feeling which she could not have achieved in any other way.

Rukmani's choice as the narrator-protagonist is also justified by the East-West theme or the tradition versus modernity theme of the novel with which the theme of poverty is interwoven. While the attitude of acceptance and resignation is pervasive in India, it is most deeply entrenched in women, particularly village women. Rukmani belongs to a village in the interior, about a hundred miles away from the town, which has remained unaffected by changes in the outer world. The writer's choice of Rukmani therefore gives her a good opportunity to show how a conservative peasant consciousness reacts to change. Change comes into Rukmani's life from several sources— from the tannery which comes 'blasting its way' into the village and effects a metamorphosis in the rural economy, from the West represented by an English missionary doctor, Kennington or Kenny, and from Rukmani's own children. The narrative device enables the writer to capture the changes brought about by the advent of the tannery and also the mixture of awe, admiration and mystery with which a simple peasant woman views a foreign doctor-benefactor.

Like Val's mother in *Possession* Rukmani and her husband belong to a generation, "thoroughly conditioned and ground into acceptance."[3] And though she is not as acquiescent as Nathan, she believes in the inevitability of suffering for those who live by the land: "Want is our companion from birth to death, familiar as the seasons or the earth, varying only in degree. What profit to bewail that which has always been and cannot change?"[4] A constant refrain with her is: "We are in God's hands" (p. 80). The limitations of such an attitude are self-evident and though the novel is written from Rukmani's point of view we are not asked to identify ourselves with it. In fact her attitude of passive acceptance is thrown into high relief by being constantly called in question in the novel. The most persistent questioning comes from Kenny who speaks for the author's own attitude: he is sympathetic yet is highly critical.

Kenny's is the voice of modernity in the novel and the writer uses him to comment on several aspects of the Indian scene—lack of planning, large families, orthodox sexual morality, the wasteful use of cowdung for fuel but most of all on the Indian attitude to suffering. He is appalled by the spectacle of Indian poverty— "your eternal, shameful poverty" (p. 71) as he calls it—and still more by the Indian attitude of unprotesting resignation to it. In his impatience he calls Indians 'meek suffering fools,' and 'acquiescent imbeciles' and contests Rukmani's view that suffering cleanses the human soul: "There is no grandeur in want—or in endurance" (p. 113). The novelist actually brings Rukmani and Kenny face to face and their opposing attitudes are highlighted when they argue for their respective points of view. The novel obviously leans towards Kenny but the discussion is inconclusive with Rukmani holding on to her point of view.

Kenny's criticism is on an ideological plane and does not alter the course of Rukmani's life. But the revolt against the traditional mores staged by the younger generation is action-oriented and influences the fortunes of the family directly. Rukmani's sons and daughter are acutely conscious, as Rukmani and Nathan are not, of the imperatives of the new situation—that the land laws are unjust and that it is futile to labour on land that is not one's own, that the land cannot support everyone in the family, that there is need to protest against socio-economic injustice, and that one must work to alleviate human suffering. Even the docile Ira who has borne her abandonment by her husband with resignation is impelled to act in defiance of traditional morality. Like Sonia in *Crime and Punishment,* Ira takes to sacrificial prostitution in order to feed her starving brother ("Tonight and tomorrow and every night, so long as there is need.", p. 99). This sobversion within the family points to a recognition of the need for change and is a hopeful sign in the novel. Rukmani reacts to these pressures for change in her own orthodox way. Since she has felt all these pressures on her pulse, her narration imparts strength and veracity to the East-West theme.

The inadequacy of Rukmani's response to the changes in her life is patent. Among other things she shows no awareness of the operation of the exploitative socio-economic system of which her family is a victim. Yet for all her limitations she never once loses the sympathy of the readers. The writer in fact ensures credence for her narrative by building her up as a simple, innocent character who faces the impossible odds in her life full face and who is, above all, generous. The generosity of her spirit is reiterated at several points in the novel. Three examples of it may be cited. Ira has been abandoned by her husband for barrenness but after Rukmani's efforts to persuade him to take her back fail she tells Ira: "You must not blame him. He has taken another woman" (p. 61). The tannery has claimed three sons of hers—one of them is a victim of its ruthless, lathi-wielding guards—but she is too fair to blame it for all her misfortunes. But she is most charitable when the family suffers the cruelest blow—eviction from the land which they have ploughed for thirty years: "This hut with all its memories was to be taken from us, for it stood on land that belonged to another. And the land itself by which we lived. It is a cruel thing, I thought" (p. 135). And then in one simple memorable sentence that recalls Christ's words in St. Luke 23:34 she forgives the absentee Zamindar all his cruelty and inhuman greed: "They do not know what they do to us" (p. 135). One could not ask for a more sensitive, honest and objective reporter. Rukmani in fact emerges from the novel as a gentle suffering soul, "a Mother of Sorrows", as K. R. Srinivasa Iyengar calls her, (somewhat like Maurya in Synge's *Riders to the Sea*) who embodies the Indian attitude of acceptance and endurance in both its weakness and strength.

The picture of poverty that the novel presents is pretty grim. As the title of the novel suggests, the fruit of the peasant's labour goes either to the landlord or is destroyed by the ravages of nature. Even Ira's 'labour' on behalf of her younger brother comes to nothing, for Kuti dies. *And yet not all the nectar seeps through the sieve.* Apart from the strength of personal relationship between Rukmani and Nathan the novel ends in hope symbolized by Selvam. Besides Kenny, he is the only character in the novel whose attitude is scientific and forward-looking. When Rukmani and others are ashamed of Sacrabani's albinism, he simply says that it is just "a matter of colouring" (p. 121). The hospital which both Kenny and he are building is complete when Rukmani starts reliving her troubled life in her imagination. And Puli's leprous hand has been cured. Since she has resisted change all along, it is significant that she should view the new building as the symbol of "men's hopes and pity" (p. 1). The hospital is the result of careful planning and a consuming desire to reduce human suffering and Rukmani's gesture of looking at the hospital building with satisfaction and pride can be taken to point to the future.

The story is told in the first person by Rukmani in retrospect. When the novel opens she is already back from her disastrous visit to the town in search of her third son, Murugan. Though she has suffered so much and has lost her dearly loved husband, she has remained unembittered. She has in fact achieved a measure of peace and serenity which give her a sense of balance as she looks back at her past. This is reflected in the fluidity of the narrative and more particularly in the controlled manner in which the painful memories are described. It is as though the distancing involved in the retrospective method had taken the sting out of the pain. There are three deaths in the family—Raja's, Kuti's and Nathan's—each one more pathetic than the other. All three are vividly and movingly described but there is no attempt to linger on them. Raja's death is a fine example of this underwriting:

> He was not very strong, they told me. They merely laid hands on him, and he fell. As if I did not know how thin and brittle he had grown! But why should others lay hands on him? They told me, but the sense of their words escaped. They told me, but I could not remember. They repeated themselves again and again, but I kept forgetting (p. 89).

With the simplest of words the writer brings out the dazed state of a mother's mind that refuses to comprehend the reality of her son's death.

A particular feature of Rukmani's retrospective narration must be mentioned. Though her narration is in the past tense, some of the scenes recalled are so clearly etched on her mind that she unconsciously switches in mid-scenes to the present tense. The scene of Raja's death is one such memory. Soon after the words quoted above, she shifts to the present tense:

> Already I think, the eyes must be closed, though death has glazed them, and I do so; the jaw must

> be tied for it is sagging, I put a bandage about it; the body must be washed and I wash it; ... (p. 90).

The narrator resorts to this switching of tenses on a few other occasions also to indicate particularly obsessive memories. Another such memory is Rukmani and Nathan's forced departure for the town in search of their son Murugan after their cruel eviction from the land. The peasant is so tenaciously attached to his land—even if he is merely a tenant—that the experience of being uprooted from the land is likely to linger long in Rukmini's mind:

> The morning of our departure comes. It is a still morning, hazy, dewy for it is yet early... The cart is piled high with bales of tightly-packed skins, for we are passengers on a return journey, but there is room enough for two... Then it is time to go... The hut—its inhabitants—recedes behind us... Our beloved green fields fall away to a blur, the hut becomes a smudge on the horizon... We are farther away with every turn of the wheels (pp. 130-40).

The memories recalled by Rukmani are graphically presented. But in one important scene one has the impression that the retrospective method gives the scene a synoptic touch diminishing the tension in it. The scene in question is one in which Rukmani discovers Nathan's adultery. After reporting her initial shock and her husband's confession, Rukmani sums up her feelings thus: "Disbelief first; disillusionment, anger, reproach, pain" (p. 86). She says what she feels but gives the readers no direct experience of her feelings. Incidentally this is one of the two scenes in which there is drama, the other scene being the discovery of Ira's prostitution. In the absence of direct depiction this crucial scene rich in irony and built up to provide high drama ends with a whimper. This is an obvious flaw, for not even Rukmani devoted though she is to her husband is likely to let go her erring husband so easily. We are left to conjecture if the brief description reflects the brevity of her bewilderment and the ease with which she is reconciled with her husband. Or is it another instance of her philosophy of acceptance and charity?

The fact that a peasant woman is the narrator inevitably raises the question of the credibility of her narration in English. How are we to accept that Rukmani should write with what Meenakshi Mukherjee calls "the smooth, uniform ease of public school English?"[5] Not only that. The novel has a South Indian setting and most of the characters have South Indian names but Kamala Markandaya writes neutral English that has no local or regional touch. Moreover, all the characters use the same style and their speeches are not individualized. This does strain the credibility of Rukmani's narration. The problem of style in Indo-Anglian writing is complex and is indeed inherent in the Indo-Anglian situation—"how to convey through English, situations, moods and expressions that are essentially Indian?"[6] So far as this novel is concerned it can be argued that accepting a peasant woman as a narrator is a matter of initial suspension of disbelief. After all we also accept the fact that all the characters, highly educated and illiterate alike, talk in English. Once, therefore, we accept the initial unreality of the situation, the merit of Kamala Markandaya's style starts becoming clear.

Nectar is written in a simple, unadorned prose which well accords with the simple, unassuming nature of the narrator-protagonist. The writing is no doubt self-conscious at times. In the first chapter itself Rukmani recalls what she as a child had said to her parents: "I shall have a grand wedding. Such that everybody will remember when all else is a dream forgotten," and then adds parenthetically: "I had heard this phrase in a storyteller's tale" (p. 2). Occasionally, the writer forgets the distinction between the narrator and herself and makes her say things that are incompatible with her rustic simplicity. For instance, Rukmani tells Kunthi that if she had a touch of the earth in her breeding,"Your values would be true" (p. 46). Sometimes she uses imagery that betokens a sophisticated mind. Two examples could be given:

> ...but we none of us said anything, for we had woven about us a net of silence in whose meshes were precariously held our fears and our despair (p. 124).

> My being was full of the husks of despair, dry and lifeless (p. 135).

Most of Rukmani's images, however, are such as generally

fall within her range of experience. Ira to her is "A maiden like a flower" (p. 34). Nathan weakened by lack of food is "as thin and dry as a hollow bamboo stick" (p. 100). At times she can startle us by using images that are particularly vivid. After the disappointment of not being able to find Murugan in the town, she describes their plight thus: "Wide, wide world but as narrow as the coins in your hand. Like a tethered goat, so far and no further" (p. 167). The first image has a muffled echo of Coleridge's *Ancient Mariner*. The second has the smell of soil in it. Much the same can be said about Rukmani's comparison of Ira's albino child to "a white crow in a flock of black..." (p. 126). These homespun images help in establishing the Indian sensibility of the narrator and contribute their share in evoking the atmosphere of an Indian village in the novel.

Nectar is the first of ten novels that Kamala Markandaya has written and anticipates several of them in both technique and theme. *Nectar's* first person narrative technique is used in *Some Inner Fury* (1955) and *Possession* (1963) and in both, the narrators are female characters. In *Some Inner Fury* the narrator is a central character Mira who, like Rukmani recalls the turbulent events of her life after a lapse of time, whereas in *Possession* the narrator is a comparatively minor character, Anusuya and she tells the story as it happens.

Nectar's theme of poverty is explored again in what is probably Markandaya's best novel, *A Handful of Rice*

(1966) but in the context of city life. Its other theme—the East-West encounter is a major preoccupation with her and she deals with different aspects of this kaleidoscopic theme in almost all her novels. The evil behind the benevolent facade of the West is the subject of *Possession* (1963). The possibilities of Indo-British relationships on a personal level are explored in novels like *Some Inner Fury* (1955), *Possession* (1963), *The Coffer Dams* (1969) and *The Nowhere Man* (1972).

Kamla Markandaya is one of the most distinguished women novelists on the Indian scene. Though she is not a didactic novelist, her work is inspired by a crusading spirit for the welfare of humanity and the alleviation of human suffering. Whatever the differences of theme and setting and style there may be in her novels, a single thread binds them together—they are what she herself calls "literature of concern."[7] Of such literature *Nectar* is a fine example.

Notes

1. Kamala Markandaya, "Reminiscences of Rural India," in *John Kenneth Galbraith Introduces India* (New Delhi: Vikas, 1974), quoted in *Kamala Markandaya* by Margaret P. Joseph (New Delhi: Arnold-Heinemann, 1980), p. 107.
2. Krishna Baldev Vaid, "The Modern Indian Novel: Some Basic Questions'" *Literary Criticism: European and Indian Traditions,* ed. C.D. Narasimaiah, quoted in *Kamala Markandaya,* by Margaret P. Joseph, p.80.
3. Kamala Markandaya, *Possession* (London: Putnam, 1963), p. 168.
4. Markandaya, *Nectar in a Sieve,* Indian rpt. (Bombay: Jaico, 1978), P. 113. All further references to this text are indicated by page numbers within parenthesis.
5. Meenakshi Mukherjee, *The Twice Born Fiction* (New Delhi: Heinemann, 1971), p. 175.
6. *Ibid.,* p. 181.
7. Quoted in *Kamala Markandaya,* p. 215.

KHUSHWANT SINGH: *Train to Pakistan*

Prafulla C. Kar

History has always provided a staple context for fiction, but a novelist takes a great risk while depending on it for structuring his fictional narrative; the risk seems greater when that history includes a part of the novelist's life. Although history invests fiction with what Henry James calls 'solidity of specification,' over-dependence on it will limit the novelist's perspective and cripple his vision. And when a novelist exploits a history that is not too distant, he tends to burden his narrative with factual irrelevancies and to turn his fiction into documentary. In the welter of facts history is likely to lose its philosophical significance. History can be a useful context only when the novelist knows how to *constitute* it properly in the frame of his narrative. The raw, unprocessed material of history gets refined in the crucible of fiction where it acquires the properties of an allegory. At this stage, history can provide to the novelist what Hayden White calls a 'poetic presence.'

A good novelist uses historical material to the extent it is quintessential to this fiction. He takes from history broad ideas and patterns and blends then into his narrative in such a way that they become a part of his fictional world. History loses its circumstantiality and becomes a timeless presence in fiction. Dickens employs the French Revolution in such a way in his *A Tale of Two Cities* where the context of history is fictionalized to serve an archetypal function without intruding into the narrative as an external agent. In other words, Dickens puts history into greater use by re-contextualizing it in his novel. Milan Kundera, the dissident Czech novelist has always used contemporary history involving totalitarianism in this way. In his fiction history is present as a transcendent phenomenon casting a long shadow on his characters. His characters are conscious of its pervasive influence and they try to escape its effect through 'jokes' and 'laughter.'[1] But the dragon of totalitarianism is too strong for them. By subjectivizing history, Kundera turns it into a useable context for his fiction.

Raymond Federman suggests that history is ultimately fictional. He evolves a pattern of human destiny from his individual experience and turns his own history into a hallucinatory phenomenon involving all of mankind. In his autobiographical novel, *Two-fold Vibration*, he meditates on history as a continuing presence. He seems to think that history turns into the supernatural when the novelist evokes it as an aesthetic phenomenon affecting the nature of narrative. Salman Rushdie also reflects on history in a similar way. In his *Midnight's Children* he makes history a fantasy. By selecting some broad events from Indian history and placing them in a spatial context, he shows that history moves systematically into apocalypse.

Many Indo-English novelists, who have used events from Indian history for shaping their narrative, have not been able to conceive of a pattern emerging from individual events. They have either narrowed down their scope by using them as mere backdrop for their fiction, or have exaggerated their roles so that they threaten to swallow their fictional context; in either case they have not given them the character they deserve. The partition of India in 1947 into two halves—India and Pakistan—has caused a big dent in the Indian literary consciousness, similar to the one the holocaust had caused in the Jewish consciousness, but only a very few novelists have successfully manipulated the event for evolving a deeper conception of history; most are journalistic in their treatment of facts. Some novelists, who actually suffered due to the partition, have used the incident as aesthetic compensation for their loss; those who did not suffer have used the occasion as a watershed in history to suggest that fiction can re-live the event which history tends to distort. Although the event has generated a tremendous creative upsurge, it has not yet produced a single novel which can compare with any of Kundera's or Federman's.

It is surprising that no novel in English by an Indian about the partition was written until 1956, the year Khushwant Singh's *Train to Pakistan*[1] was published as *Mano Majra*. Since then there has been a continuous flow of novels about the event. Attia Hosain's *Sunlight on a Broken Column* came out in 1961; Manohar Malgonkar's *A Bend in the Ganges* in 1964; Raj Gill's *The Rape* in 1974; Chaman Nahal's *Azadi* in 1975; H.S. Gill's *Ashes and Petals* in 1978; Kartar Singh Duggal's *Twice Born, Twice Dead* in 1979; V.N. Arora's *Sons and Fathers* in 1983. Most of these novels depict only the magnitude of violence and tend to be melodramatic; some like *Azadi* and *Sons and Fathers* are produced out of a nostalgic need for fictional treatment of a history which is too personal to forget. Most have tried to be truthful to the experience without trying to treat history as a fictional metaphor. Since most of them have apparently gone to the same source for factual details, C.D. Khosla's *Stern Reckoning: A Survey of the Events Leading up to and following the Partition of India* (1949), they have been tempted to use the images and motifs suggested by Khosla without trying to create new ones.

In this essay I shall try to show that, despite its many technical lapses, *Train to Pakistan* is a major breakthrough as a historical novel in Indo-English fiction. The partition serves both as a background and a foreground to the novel's vision. The action of the novel centres round a tiny village called Mano Majra on the Indo-Pakistan border during the partition. Singh weaves a narrative around life in this village, making the village a microcosm representing a larger world. Though dominated by the Sikhs, Mano Majra has as its inhabitants the Hindus and Muslims too.

Singh does not deal with the effect of the partition on the entire country; he is only concerned with how this village is transformed as a result of the partition. The chief protagonist of the novel is the village itself. Singh says that "the partition theme was born out of a sense of guilt that I had done nothing to save the lives of innocent people and behaved like a coward."[2] The novel is indeed about the sense of guilt weighing heavily on the conscience of the community as well as of the individuals. Reviewing the book in *The New York Herald Tribune Book Review,* R.H. Glauber says: "Individuals redeem themselves, but the weight of guilt remains in the community."[3] Although Singh has not been personally affected by the partition in a major way, by being a Sikh and a Punjabi he could not possibly escape from the sense of guilt resulting from his awareness of the role played by the Sikhs in the communal frenzy. Like Hawthorne tormented by guilt for the sins of his ancestors and writing about the excesses of Puritanism as a way of exorcising the demon of guilt from his conscience, Singh writes about the excesses of the partition perhaps for a similar need for purging his guilt.

Singh envisions broader patterns of history within the limited scope of the narrative, and, therefore, his novel transcends the physical world where history and fiction join in a symbiotic relationship. He suggests that behind the large-scale massacre and violence, loot and arson, a broad pattern of human behavior is discernible, and the novel indeed progresses systematically towards this awareness. The four sections of the novel—Dacoity, Kalyug,

Mano Majra, and Karma—are variations on a single theme, but each section foregrounds the action of the next and moves the story forward to a deeper vision. The sections constitute the linear movement of the narrative from depicting an apparently organically-conceived world to a world dissolving in a maelstorm; they also connect the episodes in a spatial way by suggesting the simultaneous occurrence of many incidents. In its vision, the novel moves from an apparent belief in order to a faith in philosophical determinism. As Mano Majra changes its character and takes part in the communal violence and joins the mainstream of history, the author reflects on the nature of human destiny and responds to the event by a philosophy of indifference, a response, which he seems to think, results from the utter brutality of the situation. Singh builds this transformation by skilfully orchestrating the narrative to its final denouement.

The novel begins with a focus on Mano Majra but slowly moves to suggest that Mano Majra transcends its geographical identity and becomes a metaphor. Its well-defined physical and psychological properties become murkier as the narrative progresses toward its end. In the cauldron of violence its distinct outlines get mixed up with the over-all atmosphere and lose their specificity. Thus there is a clear progression in the novel in the physical configurations of the setting as symbol as well as in the author's awareness of the event.

The progression in the novelistic vision gets more and more complex as we move from section to section. In the first section, "Dacoity," a major metaphor is worked out. The murder of Ram Lal by a gang of dacoits from a neighbouring village sets the tone of the narrative by suggesting an additional dimension to the event. Dacoity has caused dismemberment and has made some innocent persons scapegoats for the action. Figuratively, it stands for the political dismenberment of the country by the British government who blamed the local leaders for causing the partition. Thus an ordinary event is transformed into a powerful symbol. All the events that follow seem to have resulted from the dacoity.

Singh blends the event into the setting to suggest that the setting prefigures the event and sets atmosphere for the action. As the novel opens, Mano Majra is already disturbed by the news of communal violence in Bengal and Punjab and seems to think that God is punishing people for their sins. But despite the news, Mano Majra maintains perfect harmony and cordiality among its various communities. However, the unusual summer of 1947 suggests that all is not well in Mano Majra or elsewhere. The lack of rains intensifies further the effect of the unreality of the situation and builds an atmosphere for the forthcoming action. Thus the opening paragraph of the novel sets the pace of the narrative by joining the setting with the major theme.

Singh introduces most of the important characters in the opening section. The next day of the murder, the train unloads at Mano Majra station a group of armed policemen and a young Marxist radical named Iqbal. Hukum Chand, the Deputy Commissioner of the district also arrives in the village around the same time. The police arrests Iqbal and Jugga suspecting them for the murder. Thus the sleepy village awakes to life and slowly joins the turbulence outside. The sudden activity in the village brings history in motion and the isolation of the village gradually disappears.

In the next section, appropriately called "Kalyug," various loose ends of the narrative in the first section are tied together and tightened. The title of the section suggests that the novel has a cosmic vision. In the Hindu concept of epic time, Kalyug comes at the end of the cycle when the old order is destroyed and foundations for a new one are laid. The train that carries corpses from Pakistan to be cremated at Mano Majra suggests a symptom that the old world has died. The incident of mass cremation completely disturbs the rhythm of the village's life. There is a pall of gloom on the village. Everybody in the village takes the train as a premonition of evil times. Imam Baksh, the Mullah, who had maintained regularity in his prayer every evening, does not pray that evening. His "sonorous cry did not rise to the heavens to proclaim the glory of God." (p. 84). This disruption in the rhythm of Mano Majro's life suggests that the end has come.

The novel's eschatological vision of the world becomes stronger as the section builds various images in scenes involving mistaken identity, strange faces of the dead, mass exodus, and mutual suspicion and mistrust. The people, who were used to looking at the train passing by the village as part of their daily ritual, now fear the same as the harbinger of the dead. They continue gazing at it from their roof tops as a mysterious object bringing evil news.

The third section, "Mano Majra," takes the action to its further intensity. It is built around the image of the village in transformation. There is a perceptible change in not only the appearance of the village, but also in its awareness of the human condition. The section opens with a note on the changed climate: " . . . a heavy brooding silence descended on the village. People barricaded their doors and many stayed up all night talking in whispers. Everyone felt his neighbour's hand against him, and thought of finding friends and allies." (p. 117). This reversal in Mano Majra's situation from its earlier homogeneity to mutual suspicion corresponds to the change in the novelistic vision. As Mano Majra loses its healthy seclusion and gets embroiled in the national cataclysm, the action of the novel moves into the surreal. The Head Constable divides the village into two halves between the Sikhs and the Muslims and even succeeds in convincing the Sikhs that Muslims deserve punishment for their atrocities on their Gurus. As the mass exodus begins, the village turns into a ghastly scene. The houses of the Muslims are robbed, and ironically, Malli, who had robbed Ram Lal, is entrusted by the police to look after the property of the evacuees.

In the last section, "Karma," the irony gets heightened when the author joins together all the threads of the narrative and produces a surrealistic picture. The word Karma gives the novel a metaphysical dimension. Karma has a strange logic of its own; by rejecting the relationship between the cause and its effect, it justifies indifference and stoic resignation. Karma is deterministic. In Khushwant Singh's vision of the world, hope gives way to determinism, and therefore, it is appropriate that the novel ends with the chapter, "Karma". Perhaps Singh wants to suggest by ending the novel such that one can only explain the partition in terms of a philosophical determinism. The most important symbol in the section is that of flood. It becomes a mass graveyard as the dead bodies are thrown into it. The bloated bodies of men and animals as they float on the Sutlej create a surrealistic scene similar to the one in Picasso's *Guernica*.

Singh seems to suggest that in such an atmosphere of brutality human action is meaningless. Even a heroic act done in such a time does not carry any consequences whatsoever. In a strange reversal of roles, the anti-hero Jugga turns into a hero and the dacoit Malli becomes a custodian of the Muslim's property. The novel closes with such an ironic reversal of order. Jugga's act of sacrifice saves the lives of thousands of people, but their fate remains uncertain. Through Iqbal the author reflects philosophically on the nature of human action and on the price of freedom:

> If you look at things as they are, he told himself, there does not seem to be a code either of man or of God on which one can pattern one's conduct. Wrong triumphs over right as much as right over wrong. Sometimes its triumphs are greater. What happens ultimately, you do not know. In such circumstances what can you do but cultivate an utter indifference to all values? Nothing matters. Nothing whatever... (p. 172).

George Steiner says that the only appropriate response to the holocaust is silence; Kushwant Singh seems to think that the only appropriate response to the partition would be indifference, which is another way of accepting the idea of Karma as total surrender to a deterministic world.

By being an omniscient narrator, Singh has the freedom to enter into several characters in the novel and to view the action from shifting perspectives. He perhaps identifies more with Iqbal, the young Marxist who, in the course of the narrative, changes substantially. Iqbal's implicit desire to be a hero is perhaps Singh's own, a notion which one gathers as one observes Singh's obsessive desires and aspirations for recognition, and even for prominence. As Mano Majra changes its profile, the various characters also change themselves in the course of the narrative. Iqbal's early romantic notions about progress and revolution, which are products of his bookish acquaintance with Marxism, slowly give way to a mellower vision at the end. Earlier in the novel, he suggested that political freedom was meaningless without an economic one, but this simplistic notion about freedom based on cause-and-effect relationship propagated by the historians of progress is supplanted by a notion of philosophical determinism which counters the doctrine of progress. In a country of "muddleheadedness masquerading as mysticism," Iqbal seems to think, it is not possible to find any easy solution to problems. One can be killed in this country on flimsy grounds, like whether one's foreskin is removed or not. A person who had thought that criminals were made out of poverty and deprivation, has now come to a stage when such ameliorative visions no longer hold tenable in a country where freedom has complex dimensions of meaning. He is caught in a serious dilemma about the future of the country and about his own role: "his mind was like the delicate spring of a watch which quivers for several hours after it has been touched." Along with his illusions about progress, his notion of a hero also changes when he is afraid of facing the mob to tell them that what they are doing is immoral: "It was pointless. In a state of chaos self-preservation is the supreme duty." (p. 170). He rejects Indian philosophy and mysticism as high-faluting nonsense. A person who wanted to be a hero, now realizes that "it needs courage to be a coward." In Iqbal's reflection on history, Khushwant Singh suggests that history is ultimately regressive.

Like Iqbal, Hukum Chand too changes in the course of the narrative. A shrewd and efficient bureaucrat whose strength came out of his notion of expediency, comes to a stage when he begins to realize that his role as an administrator is irrelevant when the tide of violence is loosened and when history is taking a backward course. His sexual indulgence with the prostitute Haseena results from his desperate need to get over his feelings of nausea. He is tormented by guilt for his indulgence, but at the same time desires to have more of the prostitute as a way of gratifying his solipstic desire for individual security. In the process of his indulgence he develops love for the girl and thereby releases Jugga so that Jugga can try to rescue the train going to Pakistan from the violent mob.

Hukum Chand's sense of guilt is not just caused by having sex with a teen-aged girl of his daughter's age, but by his awareness that he has a share of responsibility for the atrocities committed in the name of freedom. As a government official who has toed the line of the politicians he seems to think that his role in the violence is not small. Like Iqbal he too thinks that the only response one could have to the event is cynicism. The night he sees dead bodies in the train piled upon each other as objects makes him so remorseful that he cannot sleep. Since then he is haunted by the image of the dead, an obsession which comes back to him from his childhood when he saw his aunt dying after delivering a dead child. He now realizes that the only absolute truth is death: "Within the dark chambers of his closed eyes scenes of the day started coming back in panoramic succession."

Train to Pakistan 101

By failing to stop the course of history in its violent turn, he resigns himself to his fate.

In his new role as a philosophical fool he develops an ironic vision towards politicians and their rhetoric. He is especially critical of Nehru's "Tryst with Destiny" speech on the eve of the freedom for its rhetoric and distance from truth. He implies in his long declamatory quibbles on the notion of "tryst with destiny" that political language needs to be purified from its pompous platitudes. Like Iqbal moving into indifference, Hukum Chand surrenders to prayer as the ultimate response to senseless atrocity committed by man on his own race. He covers his face with arms and starts to cry. Then he raises his face to the sky and begins to pray.

Since the novel is about time and change, the only metaphor that keeps the various threads of the narrative together is the train. V.A. Shahane is right that the change of the title of the novel from *Mano Majra* to *Train to Pakistan* is in keeping with the theme of the novel[4] Whereas *Mano Majra* suggests stasis, *Train to Pakistan* implies change. The train provided to Mano Majra an important function by regulating its life, and like the characters becoming transformed in the course of the narrative, gradually the function of the train also changes. Instead of serving a healthy link between Delhi and Lahore, it becomes a cause of division between the communities. It takes on a communal colour, depending on the direction of its movement, and toward the end of the novel its image is totally transformed. From a life-giving symbol it changes into a symbol of death. In the early part of the novel it served as an external agent controlling the village from a distance, but as the novel moves it becomes more and more a part of the inner world of the village. It impinges on the tranquility of the village and brings to it an atmosphere of terror.

Thus, in its setting, characterization, and symbolism, *Train to Pakistan* demonstrates Khushwant Singh's vision of history. Singh has used the context of the Partition for evolving such a vision. In *The Armies of the Night*, Norman Mailer has suggested that a novelist can correct the historian by his fine observation of human affairs. A historian tends to be literal in his delineation of events, but a novelist takes the essence from history and blends it into his fictional texture so that both fiction and history become refined in the process. Singh's multiple approaches to a single event through many characters and many strands in the narrative were perhaps something new in Indo-English fiction in the 1950's. By keeping the narrative loose and episodic, the author suggests the novel's potential for a spatial form. Kundera says in his recent *Paris Review* interview (No. 92) that a good novelist tries to "bring together different novelistic stories" to create a semblance of polyphony. Singh's novel does present such a polyphonic structure in a rudimentary way, although in the ultimate analysis it fails to satisfy us as a successful novel.

Its weakness seems to lie in its handling of point of view. An omniscient author's point of view is perhaps not appropriate for developing a philosophical conception of history. Singh could have brought the narrative under control by using first person and avoiding authorial intrusion. Since Singh enters into several characters when he wants to make a point, he seems to dilute his vision by the fluidity of his presence. The second weakness is the way the story is built into a climax. Jugga's sudden rise to a tragic height is perhaps gratuitous. There is no sufficient foregrounding in the text to suggest such a transformation. Perhaps, in Jugga's altruistic act, Khushwant Singh purges his own sense of guilt.

Notes

1. Khushwant Singh, *Train to Pakistan* (New York: Grove Press, 1956). All the page references to the text are to this edition.
2. "Compulsions to Write" in *Explorations in Modern Indo-English Fiction,* ed. R.K. Dhawan (New Delhi: Bahri Publications, 1982), p. 185.
3. R.H. Glauber, *The New York Herald Tribune Book Review* (April 22, 1956), p. 6.
4. V.A. Shahane, *Khushwant Singh* (New York: Twayne, 1972), p. 68.

R.K. NARAYAN: *The Guide*

Suresh Raichura

Rasipuram Krishnaswami Narayan (b. 1907) has been a practising writer since 1935, the year his first book *Swami and Friends* was published in London on the strength of a recommendation by Graham Greene who has been, since, a friend, admirer and 'guide' of Narayan's[1]. From that first book to the recent *A Tiger For Malgudi* (1983), this Mysore-based novelist, story writer, and essayist has had a long, illustrious career. All his twelve novels to-date, most of his stories, as also his adaptations of The *Ramayana* and *The Mahabharata* have been published in India, England and the U.S. Even the Russians have warmed, in recent years, to this sly, apparently unpretentious novelist who appears to eschew the grandiose, the spectacular, the sententious Big Statement.

Narayan has also been fortunate in a majority of his critics. The most outstanding of these are: V.S. Naipaul, Professors M.M. Mahood, Edwin Gerow, A.N. Kaul, V.Y. Kantak, and Willian Walsh: novelists Graham Greene, John Updike and Anthony Burgess. And *The Guide* (1958) has been perhaps his most popular novel with lay readers. Also, many full-length essays have been devoted to what is, by general consent, Narayan's *tour de force*.

The Guide

After such profligacy of critical attention as has been bestowed on *The Guide* in the years following its winning of the Sahitya Akademi Award (1958) and also the filming of separate Hindi and English versions based on it, what justification—indeed what forgiveness—can attend one more lucubration on it? Yet, the door to another such 'garden-variety' critical perception may have been left open owing to two considerations. First, Narayan's best critics have only made passing (although always insightful) remarks on this novel in their otherwise wide-ranging estimates of the writer's *oeuvre*.[2] Second, the run-of-the mill academic critics who have written on the novel have not totally foreclosed prospects of further exercises.

Perhaps one immediate opening into Narayan's work becomes available in the following *apercu* of N.J. Nanporia's in the *The Times of India* dated April 1, 1984:

> An interesting item in the list of the best novels since 1939 as selected by Anthony Burgess is R.K. Narayan's *Vendor of Sweets*. One hesitates to endorse Burgess's view that this novel 'sums up much of what modern India is about' but can hardly disagree with the verdict that, Narayan is 'the best of Indian writers in English'. Another puzzle: Why does not he sell well among Indians as among foreigners? Possibly because of all Indian writers he is almost wholly unburdened by politics and ideology. His novels are innocent of "messages" and, in this, are arguably un-Indian despite the Indianness of Malgudi.

While it is understandable that some Narayan apologists might have stakes in foisting a 'pure' writer on the unwary, such an ex-parte procedure must be resisted in the present phase of global theorization on the narrative act. The present essay is based on the assumption that texts are 'worldly', not 'innocent', regardless of how artfully they dissimulate their roles, functions, performances, tasks. And it is conceivable that Narayan's failure, to date, to write a successful didactic or political novel may have been due to failure of technique or realization rather than of genius or temperament. In any event, he is not an 'impersonal', 'value-free' writer but essentially an interested one.

It is said that if there is a a problemetic in *The Guide*, it is essentially a formal one, that the novel's crucial turn pivots on its 'open' ending which renders itself to plurisignificance, multivalence, ambiguity, irony, or parodox. A consensus has been established on the shaky grounds of the tentative 'closure' of *The Guide*. The novel's ending is supposed to signify Narayan's 'maturity', 'wisdom', or 'wit'. It is suggested that various hermeneutic or interpretive procedures can perhaps never entirely or satisfactorily unravel the Gordian Knot of *The Guide's* finale. Does it, in fact, rain in the Mempi Hills in the end or does Raju, enfeebled beyond reason and practical will as a result of his ordeal by fasting, merely hallucinate it? *The Guide's* 'poised' ending, which cannily refuses to privilege either a magical-myth-ritual-based conclusion or a staid, 'realist' as well as 'psychological' denouement is then celebrated as evidencing a mature *weltan-schaaung* on the part of Narayan and, hopefully underwriting him, the whole socio-cultural continuum whose literary manifestation he perhaps is, here and elsewhere. Ergo, the 'non-commital' Narayan is a pure writer whose 'negative capability' is to be accepted in good faith. And so it goes.

This essay is based on the view that the crux of *The Guide* turns not so much on its ending which, according to apologists of an 'ironic' or 'pure' Narayan constitutes the novel's high-water mark, as on that writer's skilful reconstitution of narrative elements of his *recit* toward the end of privileging a 'master-code' of pro-social, anti-individualist ideology—that is, a 'Hindu View of Life'. Incredible as it may sound, Narayan's narrative reaffirmation of the view that the world, cosmos and community are prior to the individual, his positing of the 'whole' over against the 'monadic', 'atomistic' or 'fragmented', shares a basic *weltansicht* with the Hegelo-Marxist-holist methodologist, Fredric Jameson. Jameson maintains that "the need to transcend the individualistic categories and modes of interpretation [of the narrative act] is in many ways the fundamental issue for any doctrine of the political unconscious, of interpretation in terms of the collective or associative[3].". Apparently, such a task confronts not only the interpretive or hermeneutic act, but also the writer's act of representation-narrativization. Here, a 'Hindu' Narayan, in foregrounding 'the collective or associative' over against 'the individualistic categories' is, however piquantly, at one with the 'dialectics' of the historicizing, Marxism-Hegelianism of Jameson, irrespective of how synchronic, ahistorical, mythical or conservative the Indian's work may be in the final analysis.

It is a fair conjecture that in his work—and nearly all his fiction may be ringing changes on a monomyth—Narayan appears to distrust modernization and its concomitants: economic and socio-psychological individualism, 'bourgeois progress' (even when, ironically, most of his own 'positive' values may have bourgeois provenance), 'capitalism' and its attendant 'chaos'. No wonder the Russians have thawed, in recent years, to Narayan who also probably reminds them of their own not-too-distant agrarian-pastoral past. He would almost certainly appear to them as a spokesman and relic of a 'primitive communism' or of sedimented social formations of India's autochthonous past.[4]

The 'positives' of a communal and familial life are matched, in Narayan's fictive but populated world, by the 'stability' of his imagined locale: Malgudi and its environs. The town, Malgudi—it keeps growing in size through the fiction and its surroundings are charted in sufficient functional detail to render them specific. To the town's north are River Sarayu and the Mempi Hills, to its South, Madras. Certain 'recurring' figures like Gaffur (legendary taxi-driver of Malgudi) further reinforce a sense of 'continuity'. Gaffur, like Nataraja or other recurring figures, becomes a part of the well-defined landscape; he is almost a landmark against which 'transients' like Marco and Rosie of *The Guide,* for instance, may be seen in relief. Narayan's dry, sparse Edwardian style, functional and occasionally solecism-ridden with its middle-level reaches, is 'cool', almost distancing. It is the perfect 'one-string' instrument for his theme. For he is concerned with celebrating the ordinary, sedimented, common-place life as opposed to the frenetic, cosmopolitan modern life. 'Modernity' and its concomitant 'materialism' are negatives in Narayan's world and he frequently identifies these with 'Americanism' (yet another reason why he should be popular with the Russians). James Malone, the TV producer, who surfaces toward the end of *The Guide,* is one of the many Americans who flit in and out of Narayan's later work. The writer plays off Malone's 'rootlessness', drive, initiative and cosmopolitan unconcern for the 'locals' against the simpler lives of the rustics from Mangala and also of Raju (who may have, finally, 'come home'), whose celebrated fasting has, in the first place, drawn the American to the locality.

The Guide is mostly a 'human' fable. And like most fables, it not only makes a pro-social, moral or even spiritual point but it also reflects 'on the commonsense ethics of ordinary life'. More, it borders on myth as also it records the predictability of experience and is ironic and realistic in tone, often satirical[5]. Further, it assumes a preliterate, oral, largely peasant culture and, as an apologue, it also reflects on the ethos of its middle-class writer, his hankering for what R. Palme Dutt, in *India Today* (1940), has called 'the comfort of some rock of ancient certainty'.

Intriguingly enough, *The Guide* opens on a landscape occupied by one 'rock of ancient certainty'. This is an abandoned shrine, now peopled by two of the book's main characters. Loneliness, *anomie*—these are notions foreign to this landscape and Raju (at the outset on the run) soon finds 'society' in the apparently unpromising figure of Velan.

It was an 'ideal' India, hermetically existing outside change, history, growth, and representing a 'timeless' telluric 'reality' of Antaeus-like spirits, that Narayan perhaps had in mind when he told Naipaul in London "that whatever happened, India would go on". It was "a conviction so deep it required no stressing"[6]. This conviction also signals a 'hunger for wholeness' that brooks no privatizing or fissiparous impediment. It is 'holist' in impulse and reflects what Northrop Frye has, in another context, called 'the myth of concern', as opposed to 'the myth of freedom'.[7]

The Guide, too, is concerned with its protagonist's 'home-coming'. It is, technically, the most audacious and artfully written, of Narayan's novels. It employs an intricate time-scheme that functions through several 'flashbacks' or 'dissolves' into the protagonist's past. These remembered events interact with the novel's 'present', when Raju is confined to one particular spot from where he can sally forth, only through fictional 'recalls' or, a little later, through the retelling (confessing) of the 'true' story of his life to the most importunate of his followers among the villagers, Velan. Raju meets the latter in the beginning on the steps of an ancient shrine, situated across the river from Mangala:

> Raju welcomed the intrusion—something to relieve the loneliness of the place. The man stood gazing reverentially on his face. Raju felt amused and embarrassed. "Sit down if you like " Raju said, to break the spell. The other accepted the suggestion with a grateful nod and wended down the river steps to wash his feet and face, came up wiping himself dry with the end of a chequered yellow towel on his shoulder and took his seat two steps below the granite slab on which Raju was sitting crosslegged, as if it were a throne, beside an ancient shrine. The branches of the trees canopying the river course rustled and trembled with the agitation of birds and monkeys settling down for the night. Upstream beyond the hills the sun was setting. Raju waited for the other to say something. But he was too polite to open a conversation.
> Raju asked, "where are you from?" dreading lest the other should turn around and ask the same question.[8]

Style, tone, setting, situation, personages—all these here coexist—are in a 'tight fit'. Minor 'natural' details—the word 'intrusion', the setting sun, the homing birds and animals, the *ancient* shrine, the full and coursing river, the rube's reverential attitude toward the slicker, a stranger—melt, create a packed image with a mildly symbolic undertone that nonetheless resonates with proleptic and minatory vibrations. Each of these details gains through incremental and qualitative progression in the novel. The yokel's 'reverential' air and his 'intrusion' upon Raju's 'privacy' will lead to complications in the plot; the sinking sun would apparently mark the end of the previous phase of Raju's life just as it would provide one device for measuring time through the novel. The 'coursing river' at this point clearly contrasts with the 'drying' river in the book's climactic sections just as it offers a proleptic relation with Raju's final movement 'down the steps of the river' (p. 221). Velan's return from a dip in the river here also contrasts with Raju's final sinking into the river's waters. Other, perhaps less 'spatial', details complete the picture. Raju's present phase of loneliness; his essentially gregarious, 'dialogic' temperament; his vacillation between a mood of extreme self-consciousness and a calmer sense of detachment; his easy assumption of social caste, superiority; his sense of decorum and rectitude; his consummate touch in mimicry ('Raju was sitting cross-legged, as if it were a throne besides an ancient shrine'); his inward feeling of uncertainty in a new, not-yet-fully-tested environment resulting in his going off at half-cock or being on the *qui vive*, especially because he appears to be intent on concealing his past—all these specifics present a thorough picture of the 'Guide'.

The die is now cast—the rest of *The Guide's mythos* would be centred on the *Karmic* unfolding of Raju's erstwhile existence. Raju's more immediate doubt and distrust of the villager at this point will make way for an opposite, trusting attitude later on, when he will voluntarily recount his 'past' to Velan, albeit in yet another futile bid to wriggle out of the narrative 'plot' and save his skin. Apparently, distrust of the other is, in *The Guide*, the obverse of lack of faith in oneself. Thus, in the novel's concluding paragraph, Raju would seem to have whole-heartedly committed himself to fasting and 'faith'. Consequently, "they held him as if he were a baby" (p. 221): Velan and the others prop up an emaciated Raju in his final 'descent' to the river as if they were re-enacting a timeless drama or ritual, *collectively* played out. Appropriately, Raju half descends, is half carried down, to the river. "The morning sun was out by now, a great shaft of light illuminated the surroundings", and the 'lonely place' of the beginning is now peopled by a crowd which "followed him down" (p. 221). In the beginning was the end for Raju and the 'ancient shrine' has perhaps been, in the end, revived, rejuvenated, by the 'blood' of a new saint. Approbative phrases like 'the swami' and 'the sage' are frequently invoked, almost ritually, in the last few pages of *The Guide*. Mangala has, hopefully but almost accidentally, found a patron saint. Will hagiolatry follow?

William Walsh, reading *The Guide* from a different perspective, finds in its ending projected 'two of Narayan's deepest convictions about human life. In the first place is his sense of the way in which at every stage of his life, the isolated individual faces the enormous, fundamentally indifferent crowd. . . "Unmitigated loneliness" and "the babble of the crowd"—it is this in the end that we feel in Raju as he stands up to his knees in the water at extreme of his strength, of his consciousness and even of his life'. Walsh further notes:

> For Narayan, then, the very conditions of human growth are individual discrepancy and communal collaboration.
>
> It is this double insight which the career of Raju embodies and justifies. At its conclusion the confidence man has become the man deserving confidence. He stands at the end up to his knees in water utterly isolated from the enormous crowd, and yet it is his collaboration—uneasy, desperate and finally total—with the expectations of the people that turns their immense illusion into something like the truth. And a faint suggestion in the last words of the novel that rain may be on the way is Narayan's method of suggesting that there is some measure of objectivity of endorsement by reality, in Raju's transformation. It has the approval of the gods of life.[9]

In Raju's undertaking of the fast Walsh finds realized the novel's identity theme: "Now at last his will matches his receptivity, the inner pattern and outer events flow together"[10] The Protean whose 'fate' it was to be the product of other people's convictions, to have a deep imitative responsiveness to persons and situations to almost an extreme degree of accommodation, finally firms up his will enough to win 'the approval of the gods of life'. The blurred line between 'sincerity and self-deception' is irretrievably erased and the novel, in Walsh's estimate, closes on an upbeat but also muted note. And life goes on even as the saints come marching in, always on the right 'number'. The 'actor' has hopefully turned 'spiritual activist', qualifying for 'sacrilization' if not 'canonization'.

Although the criminal-turned-saint is a recurring figure in Hindu mythology—Valmiki is one such—a 'saint' like Raju 'simply happens almost like the weather' (perhaps in response to phylogenetic compulsions) as the *Time's* review of the novel has said. Raju merely serves as a conduit of the possibilities of affirmation, life, implicit in his culture and is, possibly, 'different' from his 'captive audience', the *volk* of Mangala, not in kind but in degree. Yet, Raju, 'slowly sagging down' in the river at the end, remains an enigma. It is not entirely apparent, from the evidence adduced, that the individual and the community have, in fact, finally merged, become identical, or even that there is 'some measure of objectivity, of endorsement by reality in Raju's transformation'. However, most signs point toward an affirmation in the end; the stand-off at this crucial juncture almost 'freezes' the novel. Either subtlety, canniness, incompetence, ironic 'realist' awareness or plain cussedness blurs, somewhat, the ending. It is at this point that the observation made earlier in this essay will bear reiteration: the crux of *The Guide* lies in Raju's 'home-coming', not in its celebrated 'closure'.

Thus, the novel gradually, meticulously and subtly unfolds through notation of details that goes a long way toward reinforcing a sense of Raju's 'buried life'—potentialities for self-recovery which are implicit in the culture of which he is a single node. Walsh's rhetoric concerning 'some measure of objectivity of endorsement by reality' might read beautifully *per se* but his *apercu* would also appear to set great store by the 'objective' criterion of 'success' or 'heroic triumph' and would, therefore, seem a little inapposite to the stark context. *The Guide's* ending is not a 'high-water mark' but merely a consummation or confirmation of possibilities incipient in the beginning. Raju 'must change' his life but he can do so strictly in terms of the imperatives and the ensemble or repertoire of roles available to him *within* his culture.

The recourse, here, to 'theatre' imagery is to confirm its presence as a motif in *The Guide*, along with other kinetic or motile images of closing and opening of doors, spatial images of ascent or descent, rise and fall, or earthier images of eating, ('Food' imagery almost compulsively, fills up not only *The Guide* but also Narayan's latest fable of 'transformation'—*A Tiger For Malgudi*). To a degree, Raju is a chameleon, readily acclimates himself to his changing environments—first as 'Railway Raju', then as Rosie's somewhat colourless paramour, and still later as her impressario; subsequently as a prisoner (in jail, he wholly expectedly turns into a 'model prisoner'). And, to crown all his previous roles- the 'regal' motif is also present in the novel—he finally assumes, in the 'present' of the novel, the role of a holyman.

Thus, in the beginning, there is "the granite slab on which Raju was sitting cross-legged, as if it were a throne, beside an ancient shrine" (p. 5). The as-yet impostor here strikes an appropriate posture. Narayan from here goes on to develop points of contrast between not only Raju and Rosie but also between the guide and Marco, the 'stranger' and Velan, and between Raju and the other characters.

A narrative system of parallels, similarities and contrasts becomes an enabling device for Narayan to tie up various strands of his story and to weave a seamless 'historiçal' fabric. As Walsh has noted, 'Rosie and Raju are two of a kind and they fall in love at once'.[11] Just as Rosie hits the high time when Raju, evincing 'faith' in her terpsichorean talent, undertakes to 'manage' her, thus assisting her gradual elevation to stardom, Velan, manifesting a 'reverential' attitude toward Raju in the beginning of the novel's 'present', catapults the guide toward a situation of no return. (The novel repeatedly alludes to Raju's growing circle of admires, fans, to his 'audience'.) Again, Raju himself takes a calculated, 'actor's', risk when he makes his first overture to Rosie after he has realized that there is an 'opening' for him owing to marital discord between Marco and her. 'Trying on Marco's behalf,' becoming 'bold'; he has his first independent speech with the divine creature, Rosie.[12] Even in retrospect—when he is telling his life-story to Velan—Raju can barely conceal his ardour. Yet, in actuality, Raju's romantic naivete is tempered by deliberate cold-bloodedness as, on the subject of Marco and Rosie's conjugal love, he has played a hunch. Simultaneously, what he says here—sincerity and self-deception being so mixed in him—has as much bearing on his short-term 'future' with Rosie in his recalled 'past' as it has in relation to the novel's 'present', which inexorably moves toward an ending. Here, the novel's two plots are spliced:

> I might either make a fool of myself or win the heavens. How should I announce myself? Would she know my famous name? (p. 64).

This provincial does 'win the heavens' with Rosie but only for a while—*sic transit gloria mundi*. The sequel to his affair of the heart deals not only with 'the End of the Affair' with Rosie but also with the apparently 'Burnt Out Case,' Raju's 'announcing' of himself or, alternatively, with the world's suddenly, 'knowing' of his 'famous name'—'the Heart of the Matter' being Raju's rediscovery of a spiritual 'Power and Glory'. The story of Raju 'the saint' is at once like and unlike the story of the Secret Life and Good Times of Raju Guide and all those who had crossed his path—Rosie, Marco, Gaffur and many others.

After the collapse of his 'show' with Rosie and his consequent imprisonment, Raju finds himself back at square one. At this juncture, he wanders off toward Mangala, still at a loose end, vaguely unsure about a new 'career'. Velan unwittingly becomes the 'agent' who 'launches' Raju's 'new career'. Here is a 'new life'. Raju's common-sense obvervations, spoken 'grandly' (p. 15) are grasped by Velan as oracular truths. (Two figures—one educated, 'American' or 'Western' and the other a salt-of-the earth rustic, apparently 'illiterate'- repeatedly square off in Narayan's *oeuvre*; this fictive *pas de deux* leading to a stand-off of mutual incomprehension; ironic 'misunderstanding') Raju's invocation, at this juncture, of the Buddha ('the enlightened one' who, too, had once been a sensual man of the world) is 'natural'; he takes delight in talking through conundrums. Yet, it is by his retelling of Hindu mythological tales— ones he had learned in his childhood from his mother— to his naive audience that he comes to feel his way toward his real 'home'. For he too has probably 'come, trailing clouds of glory'.

However, his transformation is gradual and painful. In the early stages, when Velan 'tried to touch Raju's feet', the guide 'recoiled at the attempt' and promptly upbraided the villager. Concurrently, he also 'felt he was attaining the stature of a saint' (p. 15). Again, when Velan agrees to fetch his step-sister to Raju for 'spiritual' counsel, the Old Adam stirs in the guide but briefly and nostalgically.[13]

On his first evening by the ancient shrine after Velan's

departure. Raju is, once again, alone and not yet alone, for cosmic mysteries engulf him:

> He sat there for a long time watching the river flow into the night, the rustle of the peepul and banyan trees around was sometimes loud and frightening. The sky was clear. Having nothing else to do, he started counting the stars. He said to himself. "I shall be rewarded for this profound service to humanity. People will say, 'Here is the man who knows the exact number of stars in the sky. If you have any trouble on that account you had better consult him. He will be your night guide for the skies.'" He told himself, "The thing to do is to start from a corner and go on patch by patch. Never work from the top to the horizon, but always the other way." He suddenly realized that if he looked deeper a new cluster of stars came into view: by the time he assimilated it into his reckoning, he realized he had lost sight of his starting point, and found himself entangled in hopeless figures. He felt exhausted. He stretched himself on the stone slab and fell asleep under the open sky (pp. 15-16).

That concluding 'under the open sky' is, in part, a sly reminder that Raju has been, until recently, a jail-bird. The guide, at this point, is yet a fantasist and also a man of schemes (as Rosie and Marco, too, had been creatures of 'plans'). Concurrently, he is adaptable to any surrounding and always manages to find work for himself; old habits die hard. Narayan then places this single node of consciousness (which, however insignificant it may be in relation to the whole of the circumabient cosmos, is yet 'significant' for itself) within the context of a universe that almost mocks at anthropocentric meanings. Yet this is the base-line from which Raju will progress toward self-recovery, 'patch by patch', toward a realization that 'if he looked deeper, a new cluster of stars came into view,' unto infinity. These are stars other than Rosie, Marco, Raju, or the 'Star Lawyer from Madras' who deigns to plead for Raju after the latter's arrest.

But to proceed, Raju must back-track, painfully traverse vast stretches of his past life, if only to retrace and perceive a pattern in what has gone before. Only thus can there be an 'end' implicit in the 'beginning'. Part of Raju's spiritual self-therapy might lie in making his past accessible and public in the present through the retelling of it even if to only one person, the old faithful Velan, who "was made of the stuff disciples are made of" (p. 17). Narayan neither blinks nor stints other 'realistic' details. For instance, the villagers are far from being ideal pastoral types. But these 'facts' merely reinforce, even if only by contrast, the theme which is concerned with Raju's realization of his own 'importance' in the nature of things or, at least, within the dispensation of the Hindu view of life.

Many incidental details help toward realizing *The Guide's* ethos and *gestalt*, contribute toward 'congruence-building'. For instance, it is through the agency of his mother that Raju has, however subliminally, grasped the culturally significant identity elements which will initially assist him in surviving at a practical level as a story-teller-cum-medicine-man amidst the rustics and finally prepare him for his 'transformation' and 'sainthood'. Gaffur, Marco, the chatty barber Raju first encounters on his release from jail, the typed school-master, the 'adjournment lawyer' and the 'Star Lawyer from Madras'; Rosie's secretary, Mani, Raju's irascible uncle, those among the villagers who are 'individualized'; all these contribute toward a strong chiaroscuro effect.

The Guide's narrative technique itself functions in service of the total design. Had the story been told in chronological sequence, the novel might have had two climaxes; the first, Raju's 'fall', disgrace and imprisonment and the second, his flight to Mangala, followed by the consequences of his assumption of 'saintliness'. In the event, the total impact could have been dissipated. By paring away Raju's 'inessential' past or at least by relegating it to the backward and abysm of time, Narayan gains in concentration, focus, pattern and significance. Hence, the novel begins at the point where Raju is tentatively poised toward 'a new life'. Consequently, his recalled past merely serves as a stepping-stone in his ascent toward a new 'career'. The novel's 'flashback' or total-recall technique also serves as an enabling device for Raju to take stock of his life (this hopefully helping him toward overcoming those weaknesses which had implicated him in his past), to grasp the basic but also dynamic pattern of his life. Repeatedly, in the course of his recollections, Raju appears to believe that his affair with Rosie had somehow 'reduced' him, severed his links with his immediate community and injected into his otherwise pure bloodstream microbes of virulent mistrust and suspicion (pp. 100-107).

This particular effect is also reinforced through the book's 'spatial' imagery. When his affair with Rosie 'matures', Raju hides and shulks inside dark rooms—where he proceeds to make love to the danseuse—away from the inquisitive gaze of his erstwhile acquaintances, 'friends' or trade associates. For he then locks 'the door on the world' (p. 78). Predictably, the affair will culminate when the world will shut its door on the delinquent—it ends with Raju's incarceration. Conversely, by the 'ancient shrine', he finds himself in an 'open' relation to wide spaces and 'open' people, in fact, to the living cosmos.

Rosie herself remains, to the bitter end, an enigma for Raju, even during his disturbed recollections, as if his bafflement were an ironic counterpoint to Marco's quizzical remark to Raju in their early days: 'You have probably no notion how to deal with women, have you?' Raju's response, then made frivolously, also carries a dramatic irony: 'I have no idea' (p. 63). Rosie is, probably, among the first of many 'modern women' in Narayan's work. (And yet, she is more conventionally hide-bound, less 'emancipated' than some later ones like the ambivalently-named Grace of *The Vendor of Sweets*, 1967, or Daisy of *A Painter of Signs*, 1977). Raju's perplexity toward Rosie-turned-Nalini (her 'transformation' anticipating his own[14]) may, perhaps, reflect Narayan's as well toward 'modern women'. (Indeed, it may be worth speculating whether the modern 'rationality', pragmatism or 'disorder' embodied in Grace and Daisy, among others, and also in modern men like Marco and Sam of the story, 'A Breath of Lucifer' (1970), may not have constrained Narayan to withdraw into the certitudes of fable and myth in *A Tiger For Malgudi,* where the distraught and distracting humans are seen as if through the wrong end of a telescope: 'God, what fools these mortals be.'

Modernization—which, at least in part, is responsible for Raju's worldly 'undoing'—had come to Malgudi with the building of the town's railway station. A sleepy whistlestop on the road to Madras is gradually 'transformed' (in yet another ironic counterpoint to Raju's later 'transformation') with the laying of its brick and mortar. Raju himself, in whose early childhood this monument to modernity, change and 'progress' is being built, simultaneously 'grows' along. It is, thus, only appropriate that he should, at one point, be dubbed 'Railway Raju'. For he, like the station, is one of the evolving town's 'institutions'. Interestingly, the construction of the station is merely the thin edge of the wedge: Raju learns his first 'bad words' from the gangmen on site. In his adolescence, Raju will have found, in the hurlyburly of the station, a refuge from school and discipline. He will virtually come to bed down on its single platform after his father had bequeathed on him a concessionaire's stall there. Raju's first 'successful' career is 'launched' at this juncture. He will now begin his slow drift away from home even before the death of his father. There is also a suggestion that the station itself is virtually conjured, *ex nihilo,* as *maya,* as if to offer a prolepsis for Raju's own career, which begins on a minor scale as 'Raju Guide' and then gradually swells with his undertaking 'management' of Rosie's career. Raju will have moved even further from his moorings after a change of abode—he moves to the town's New Extension after his mother's departure to her ancestral village, this itself followed by Rosie's spectacular debut. Diametrically opposed to the town's 'modern' institutions, however, are the primeval Mempi Caves (shades of the Marabar Caves!)

The railway station will bring more trouble for Raju. One day the 'transients', Marco and Rosie, land up there because the former, an archaeologist, wants to 'do' the caves. Like many other 'satisfied' tourists Marco, too, finds in the guide a complaisant factotum if not also an eager boy scout. This is the perfect set for the latter to become embroiled in the couple's business. Finally, when things get out of hand, Marco takes the Madras train alone, leaving Rosie behind to fend for herself. Predictably, coxcomb Raju is dead ringer for a chivalric hero: he gives her a helping hand. A certain naivete (allied with 'romantic' ardour, unctuousness or plain egregiousness) drives him into an imbroglio with Rosie. Narayan deftly records the minutiae of this troubled relationship which, in Walsh's felicitous phrasing, "strikes one, as being as much a crisis of nerves as of passion".[15]

The ridiculous and the serious, the mundane and the elevated, are the ingredients of this somewhat improbable *affaire de coeur*. Its first phase 'culminates' in the preposterous events at the Peak House. (Its glassed-in observation platform separating the three humans involved in an implausible *menage a trois* from the flora and fauna about the buildings). On the face of it, after Rosie moves into Raju's ancestral home, the guide's career starts off on an upswing. But the bubble will soon burst: Raju is from now on a marked man. Predictably, his own contribution to his partly comic catastrophe is by overreaching himself. Through muddled motivation—it is, in part, his protective attitude toward Rosie-Nalini, in part jealousy of Marco— he forges a document sent by Marco for Rosie to sign for her to receive some jewellery bequeathed by the archaeologist. Expectedly, the counterfeit is spotted by Marco and his solicitor. Retribution swiftly follows, bringing to end Raju's 'chivalric' embroilment in the couple's affairs. For Raju, it is easy come, easy go. If, as in Daniel Bcorstin's wicked formulation, a celebrity is "known for being well known",[16] Raju, having simply hitched a ride on the Rosie-Nalini bandwagon, has rushed to the conclusion that he too is a celebrity. He, however, pays the price when that gig is blown. Yet another 'celebrity' career still awaits him, that of a 'saint'.

But before the novel's devout and not entirely unwished-for end transpires, before his *agon* in Mangala begins, Raju undergoes penance: a jail sentence. Here he grabs yet another opportunity to be 'of service' to others. The prison, then, is a full-dress rehearsal for Raju's perhaps more consummate, final performance as a 'model saint'. He thus progresses from rags-to riches to rags-to-robes. The role of the saint, first tried on for fun and more importantly for food, becomes a tight fit. Raju lives by the ancient shrine for three years or more before the moment of truth catches up on him. At this point, the thin dividing line between 'sincerity and self-deception' begins to blur. Like the Trotskyite ex-revolutionary Spina, who first disguises himself as a priest to elude his enemies and then gradually finds himself metamorphosed into a saint in Ignazio Silone's *Bread and Wine,* Raju, too, begins to 'change' in a manner perhaps even imperceptible to himself (sometimes also recalling yet another 'picaresque saint', the whisky-priest in Graham Greene's *The Power and the Glory).* Now an unexpected spring of 'wisdom' begins to well 'from the depths' of Raju's 'being' (p. 41).

When Raju embarks on his twelve-day fast (emulating, perhaps, a mythological saint whose tale he had once told his gawking audience), a roving journalist lights on the scoop. Soon, crowds begin to converge on the spot. As crowds increase in size, different activities are drummed up in order to 'organize' them. The district's Health Department grabs this opportunity to innoculate people; the Tea Propaganda Board pitches a tent in this coffee-drinkers' territory to provide free samplings of the beverage. Fun and games proliferate as hucksters and vendors move in for the kill: an enterprising gamester also sets up a gambling booth. Concurrently, government films are shown by mobile vans and coarse film music blares from loud-speakers on the spot. The flippant and the serious here merge (in a way vaguely reminiscent of the 'Temple' sequence in *A Passage to India*). While the resultant 'mixed tone' may redound toward diffusing and dispersing the 'tragedy' of Raju's fast-unto-death, it is also probable that such 'Audenesque' irony may contribute toward two other effects. First, by playing off the somewhat faceless and enormous crowd against Raju's singular commitment in the end, Narayan hopefully insists on Raju's spiritual growth. Second, the crowd may be, like Raju, Rosie, Marco, Velan and the others, Janus-faced. For the same jubilating crowd becomes hushed, intent, awed, when Raju finally wends his way to the river.

Other comico-serious images of 'submergence' prefigure Raju's ankle-deep immersion in the river at the end. Raju's first view of Rosie (a Janus) is wittily presented: "a complexion, not white but dusky which made her only half visible as if you saw her through a film of tender coconut juice" (p. 58). Marco is so dubbed because he reminds Raju of an 'African *Shikari*' (p. 72) and Marco's helmet and thick jacket are *transformed*, in Raju's active imagination, into sections of a deep-sea diving equipment[17]. When Rosie 'accidentally' brushed Raju at dinner in the Peak House, 'Everything disappeared into a sweet, dark haze, as under chloroform' (p.68). Raju's own recollections of Rosie also function as if in a 'sweet, dark' haze, as something seen through the glass, darkly.

The Guide, is also packed with felicities other than images of theatre, sculpture, water, 'submergence' and narcosis. Conversely, Narayan often stretches probability in this novel. Even as 'incomprehension' and its concomitant irony are active elements of the plot, even while Raju's 'incomprehensible' fate is variously prefigured in image, metaphor, rhetoric, character and event, the *deus ex machina,* the idiot boy whose misprision of the message Raju sends to Velan and the others precipitates Raju's final 'triumph' and tragedy, is, patently, a lazy after-thought or subterfuge to wind down the plot.[18] Similarly, Raju's reasons for fasting (he is afraid of the police following him to his Arcadian sanctuary) sound factitious. Perhaps it could be that Raju is too jealous of his new-found self and freedom, of his 'reputation' in his newly-adopted community to wish the police anywhere near him. It is also likely that Raju merely rationalizes, as his 'fear' of police, what is actually his evolving submission to the call of destiny. In other words, his motives for undertaking the fast remain obscure, Nonetheless, he had been a model prisoner and has been, also too wordly-wise to be afraid of the police. More, his undertaking of the fast would have an opposite effect: that of drawing the world to 'press around' on him (p. 214).

The Guide also has antecedents in Narayan's *oeuvre.* While most of his early work is by way of preparation, it is almost certain that parts of *The Bachelor of Arts* (1937) and of *An Astrologer's Day* (1947)—offer definite anticipations. Further more, *The Guide* serves as an important signpost directed toward Narayan's later work and it remains, in all probability, his most considerable achievement to-date.

Notes

1. Narayan has told Vir Sanghvi: 'It was he (Greene) who first arranged for the publication of one of my books and he has always been the first person to ready my manyscript'. Cf. 'I Find My Own Work Very Boring: Dialogue', *Imprint* (February 1984): 51. Also, Greene had, apparently, prevailed over Narayan on the matter of *The Guide's* ending. Cf. R.K. Narayan, *My Dateless Diary* Mysore: Indian Thought Publications, 1960), p. 97: 'While I was hesiating whether to leave my hero alive or dead at the end of the story Graham was definite he should die'.

2. However, William Walsh has a long essay on *The Guide* in *R.K. Narayan: A Critical Appreciation* (New Delhi: Allied, 1982) pp. 114-33. Cf., also, William Walsh, 'Sweet Mangoes and Malt Vinegar' in *Indo-English Literature: A Collection of Critical Essays*. ed. K. K. Sharma (Ghaziabad: Vimal Prakashan, (1977). See, also, William Walsh, *A Human Idiom: Literature and Humanity* (London: Chatto & Windus, (1964).

3. Fredrick Jameson, *The Political Unconscious: Narrative As a Socially Symbolic Act* (Ithaca: Cornell University Press, 1981), p. 68.
4. For gushing adulation of Narayan's use of myth and legend which renders his work 'nationalist', see a representative Russian scholar E.J. Kallinokova's 'Indian Myths and Legends in R.K. Narayan's Interpretation', *Perspectives on R.K. Narayan*, ed. Atma Ram (Ghaziabad: Vimal Prakashan, 1981). As Russian Formalists—now unpopular in their own country—might have said, Narayan 'rebarbarizes' fiction.
5. Cf. Roger Fowler, ed. *A Dictionary of Modern Critical Terms* (London: Routledge & Kegan Paul, 1973), p. 68. *The Guide*, however, is not a 'beast fable'—a category to which *A Tiger for Malgudi* should have better claims.
6. V.S. Naipaul, *An Area of Darkness* (Harmondsworth: Penguin Books, 1964), p. 216. For some incisive commentary on Narayan's fiction as what Engels has called the 'triumph of realism', see, also, V.S. Naipaul, *India: A Wounded Civilization* (New Delhi: Vikas, 1977), pp. 15-27; 36-43. 51-3. In both the early *Mr. Sampath* and the late *The Vender of Sweets*, Naipaul notices a common theme: 'there is venture into the world of doing and at the end there is withdrawal'. This *Leitmotif* recurs, *mutatis mutandis*, in *The Guide* as well.

7. Northrop Frye, *The Critical Path* (Bloomington: Indiana University Press, 1980), p. 44. Frye has a projectivist/idealist, certainly a 'humanist'/Christian bias.
8. R.K. Narayan, *The Guide* (Mysore: Indian Thought Publications, 1958) P. 5. Subsequent references to this text are made by quoting appropriate page numbers in parentheses within the main body of the present essay.
9. Walsh, *R.K. Narayan*, pp. 131, 129. Walsh's approach to Narayan's 'Hindu' or 'tragi-comic' art (in which, as Narayan puts it in *Mr. Sampath*, things may be 'neither particularly wrong nor right, but just balancing themselves') is frequently reverential, adulatory, or zealously hierophantic. Walsh argues that Narayan's 'profound Hindu conviction, or instinct for, the fundamental oneness of existence' operated 'in harmony with a quick feeling for the instantaneous present; an appreciation of the multiple and dispersed nature of existence'.
10. Walsh, *R.K. Narayan*, p. 129.
11. Walsh, *R.K. Narayan*, p. 123.
12. The *topos* of mastering the cosmopolitan 'world' by a provincial, mainly through his erotic conquest of a high-class lady, recurs in the nineteenth-century European and especially French novels of, among others, Stendhal and Balzac: Raju is Julien Sorel or Lucien Chardon *manque*. Similarly, Rosie may be a metamorphosed version of a noble woman (however,

Rosie's own 'birth qualifications' are compromised by her dubious if not depraved and low antecedents) and Marco is, perhaps, a denatured avatar of the jealous but powerful aristocrat/husband. Marco also resembles George Eliot's Casaubon and Henry James' Gibert Osmond (just as Raju may recall Caspar Goodwood, the boy scout of *The Portrait of a Lady*).

13. Cf. *The Guide,* p. 15. Raju's retrospection, his confession to Velan, abounds in self-protective gestures. Even in the end, the 'floating feeling' included by his enforced fasting appeals to the as-yet deep-dyed hedonist in him. For he 'enjoys' the sensation which he believes Velan 'cannot take away' from him.

14. Rosie's single-minded devotion to herself if not her art, her female self-sufficiency (wistfully and wrily recorded in Raju's reminiscences of her), provides one model for the ex-guide's final 'commitment'. *The Guide,* as is Narayan's other work, is preoccupied with the issue of the choice of vocation, destiny, call. Also, choice and chance combine to complete Raju's destiny. In a way, Raju described a journey from the practical ego through personal unconscious to collective unconcious.

15. Walsh, *R.K. Narayan,* p. 123.

16. Quoted by James Monaco in *How to Read a Film: The Art, Technology, Language, History and Theory of Film and Media* (New York: Oxford University Press, 1977), p. 400.

17. It is interesting that 'modern', industrial-age imagery of the diving equipment should be associated with Marco. Unlike Raju and Velan, both of whom descend to the redemptive river at various stages of the story, Marco needs to protect himself from water, 'submergence', 'oceanic feelings'. He is an egotist par excellence and his element is the rocky Cave with its 'dead' past, or the glassed-in observation room of Peak House in the Hills.

18. Even here a counterargument may be based on the view that Velan, who has from the beginning misunderstood Raju and his oracular *pronunciamentos*, is the *doppelganger* of his idiot brother, who is conjured from thin air in the novel's climax. Perhaps the confusion that the cretin generates, through his garbling of Raju's message to the villagers provides 'poetic justice': Raju who has lived by the quibble (or gift of gab) also dies by it. Perhaps his entire life has been a Comedy of Errors, a case of 'mistaken identity'. In such an ironic context, *The Guide* (if not its author as well) lives by the quibble even if the guide cannot.

MANOHAR MALGONKAR: *A Bend in the Ganges*

N.S. Pradhan

Manohar Malgonkar is one of the most under-rated writers of English novel in India. Although he enjoys immense popularity with his readers whose number is by no means small, literary critics tend to dismiss him as a historical romancer, a writer of popular fiction whose works, being devoid of serious content, merely emphasize good story-telling. It is true that novels like *Spy in Amber* and *Shalimar* (which originated as a film script) were specifically written for the popular taste. And several of his short stories have a light-hearted banter giving the impression that the author was at pains to avoid anything as unsavoury as complexity or depth or intensity of feeling, in them. It is, thus, that G.S. Amur, while comparing Malgonkar with Raja Rao, states that the former "considers himself as essentially an entertainer, a storyteller and scrupulously keeps away from metaphysics".[1] And again, while tracing John Masters' influence on Malgonkar, Amur rather unfairly and quite unnecessarily concludes that "Malgonkar's own recipe of a successful novel —a combination of sex, violence and politics—has a close correspondence with Masters' own . . ."[2] Similar other reviewers have added to this simplistic and narrow image of Malgonkar. This essay seeks to dispel some of these notions by bringing out the major social and philosophical concerns in Malgonkar's fiction, underscoring at the same time some of his artistic achievements. And if one were to depend on only one of his novels for this task there could be no better choice than *A Bend in the Ganges*.

A Bend in the Ganges (1964) was Malgonkar's fourth and most important novel, the earlier ones being *Distant Drums* (1961), *Combat of Shadows* (1962) and *The Princes* (1963). In these earlier novels, as in *A Bend,* one of the author's chief concerns is to depict the predicament of man in a world where values are changing too fast for his comprehension and adjustment. Man faces a crisis brought on by the breakdown of the old order and he feels no longer anchored to a safe tradition. In the resulting chaos some are destroyed, some flounder by the wayside and some survive on the strength of one or two lasting values which remain intact in the winds of change. Malgonkar's grasp of this eternal situation, a fact of life that puzzled the Greeks and all serious writers thereafter, at once places him at a level decidedly better than that of merely popular writers. *Distant Drums* is thus a saga of change, brought on by India's independence, in the formal and tradition-bound life in the Indian army, stiffened by ages of hard discipline and archaic rituals (ceremonial sneezing in the officers' mess, the bagpiper marching on the gravel-path every morning to awaken the Commanding Officer'). The new order is represented by the younger officers' hatred of the British, the jet set who go to the movies with notebook and pencil to learn new American expressions, the betal-chewing dhoti-clad politicians. Under the floss of some bizarre practices the old world managed to preserve discipline, decency, fellow-feeling and camaraderie. The values of new world are selfishness, crudity, vulgarity and hatred. The protagonist of the novel, a colonel, barely manages to survive, although his commitment to the values of the past is exposed to the repeated onslaught of modern and hostile pressures.

Malgonkar has often been accused of projecting 'traditional' and 'conservative' values in his fiction, making him appear as a writer out of step with the modern world.[3] In *Distant Drums* he is thought to be guilty of promoting the English public school morality as it operated in colonial India, at the expense of ignoring the new forces which had brought freedom to the country.[4] These views are misleading and tendentious: Malgonkar merely stresses the need for a life of decency, uprightness, self-respect and a moral code of conduct. To label these values as old or conservative, is, to say the least, strange: Malgonkar's moral vision has to be comprehended by delinking it from the historical boundaries of old and new. Nowhere else is this more evident than in *Combat of Shadows* whose English protagonist meets a tragic end; he, in order to pursue an ambitious career, cultivates a "new sense of values aimed exclusively at success";[5] he "discovered that it was dead easy to make a living if you eased up on your sense of values. . ."⁶ The values he abandons are composed of a commitment to honourable conduct and decency; what he acquires leads him to cheat, to beat up a defenceless woman, to viciously develop hatred and a snobbish sense of racial superiority and finally to commit a cold-blooded murder. A 'slackening of the moral fibre' is all that *Combat of Shadows* depicts with its inevitable consequences. It is, however, in *The Princes* that Malgonkar is most accused of promoting the obsolete, feudal and decadent life-style of the Indian princes. "It simply would not do to see in him (the protagonist) a modern challenge to the values of his class."⁷ Abhayraj, the young prince is seen, in the final situation, to be a champion of the old and now dying feudal system. This sort of superficial reading of the novel, as in the previous cases, deprives it of its meaning at its core. *The Princes* depicts a young man's predicament caught in the swift historical changes which saw an ancient, almost primitive social order give place to a modern democratic set up. The princes became commoners and the untouchables (as in this particular case) became rulers. Malgonkar (and his protagonists) accept this reality but mourn the disappearance of the old culture and refinement with an almost tragic awareness of the incvitability of certain losses and new gains.

The classic situation of a man beset by conflicting values brought on by external, quite often historical changes is illustrated with a rare intensity and comprehensive-

A Bend in the Ganges

ness in *The Devil's Wind* (1972), Nana Sahib, a prominent leader of the Indian Mutiny of 1857, tries to follow a life of decency, order, fairplay and truth but is forced by circumstances to lead to revolt, violence and unprecedented brutality. In consequence, he remains an intensely tragic figure who, in moments of rare objectivity, recognises the unbridgeable gulf between a gentle private self and a ruthless public duty forced on him by historical and hereditary causes. Malgonkar succeeds in convincing us that Nana Sahib whom the English believe to be a monster and the 'villain of the century' is truly a gentleman at heart who is numbed into being a mere puzzled spectator by the intricate and violent conditions of his life.

This basic pattern in the novels of Malgonkar—the individual stranded at a cross-roads and faced with a moral predicament or impelled to seek his identity—is vastly enriched by the detailed yet sweeping account of social, political and historical circumstances. In fact, so powerful and precise is his historical vision that at times his novels read like documentary, true-life accounts of the tempestuous events described. Quite often, his focus shifts from the individual to the event the presentation of which is marked by sharp detail, epic dimension and genuine authenticity. Also present is an intricate network of social relations depicting the arrogant and complacent ruling English, the middling and pathetic Eurasians, the feudal princes in their intimate palaces where intrigues and conspiracies breed, the Indian army officers trained in the culture of their English superiors, the vast Indian upper and lower middle classes with their ambitions and frustrations, the new-fangled unscrupulous politicians, the untouchables, the labourers, and the criminals. The world of Malgonkar's fiction is vast and captures the massive flux of life in India in all its richness and variety.

A Bend in the Ganges exemplifies this aspect of Malgonkar's fiction to a perfection. The panorama of life in India is painted in all its vividness. The placid life in a Panjab town, the sylvan rolling fields of Gian's ancestral village in the hills, the wild and primitive conditions at the Cellular jail on the island of Andaman, the jet-set life styles of the rich in Bombay and the cataclysmic mob violence at the end—all these create not only dramatic richness and variety in the main plot, they lend an epic dimension to the entire scene. Similarly, the action of the novel begins in 1930's and extends upto the dawn of Independence in August 1947, thus encompassing the history of a saga depicting the movement for Independence, the World War and the Partition of India.

How does Malgonkar manage to hold this disparate material together? Apart from the fact that the action is too spread out and the time-span is rather long, there is also the problem of accommodating two protagonists, Gian and Debi, in the plot. As a result, the plot appears to be complex, meandering, at times shapeless, zigzagging between the two main episodes. One feels, at times, that the plot is so supple and loose that a number of other possible episodes, for example, describing terrorist exploits or brutalities in the prison or love scenes between Gian and Sundri, could have been included without making any difference. And yet the plot has a basic unity which singularly holds together, firstly by a series of sharp contrasts and correspondences between the two protagonists and secondly, through a carefully chalked out ever-recurring pattern of betrayal and revenge in the story.

The characters of Gian and Debi are a study in contrasts. A product of lower middle-class, rather pedestrian background, Gian begins and remains as a traditional-type of person whose discarding of the Janwa (the sacred thread) early in the novel, does not instantly make him a modern man. Debi, on the other hand, is the scion of a rich artistocratic family who takes his wealth for granted. His liberated, pseudo-intellectual life-style and rather unbending pride find expression in the ceremony of eating a meal of beef and pork (alongwith the other members of the revolutionary group) not only as a symbol of his emancipation but to seal the ideal of communal harmony. Gian holds all Englishmen in high admiration and shares the lower classes' faith of the period that against the corrupt and thoroughly degenerate petty Indian officials, the English were 'fair and just.' His allegiance to the jail superintendent Mulligan, although condemned by his companions, and used by critics to suitably illustrate his 'degraded' character, has to be understood as a sociological phenomenon emanating from the innate loyalty of the underdog towards a master who is powerful and protective. Debi burns with an indiscriminate hatred for the English, having been a witness as a child to an attempted rape of his mother by a drunken English soldier. The basis of his hatred, and of his patriotic idealism, is, to some extent, personal and psychological. Gian is a more introverted person whose life, having a simple and uncomplicated beginning, is a string of questions and self-probings regarding his own true character. Was he a coward? he brooded after his brother had been killed before his eyes. And on his way to the Andaman prison, lying chained as a convict in the hold of the ship, he reflects:

> Was it his youth that made him so shallow, he wondered, or was it a part of the Indian character itself? Did he in some way, represent the average Indian, mixed up, shallow and weak? Like someone out of *A Passage to India*, Aziz, or someone even more confused, quite despicable, in fact, like that boy whose name he had forgotten, Rafi, that was it . . . ' (128).

Debi, all along, is steady and unchanged in his self-image, his convictions, his high idealism and his hatred. Gian has no thought of leaving the Andamans and thinks of making his permanent home there since he has nothing to go back to. Debi is forever thinking of escape in order to fulfil his mission of life. Even in their attitude towards violence, initially atleast, there is a sharp contrast. From being a follower of Gandhi, Gian's faith in non-violence is genuinely felt although it breaks when put to a severe test. Debi has deliberately cultivated the cult of violence as a means of achieving the noble end of throwing the English out from India. It is only in this regard that both Gian and Debi have something in common as, in the later stages of the novel, they get confused in their view of violence. These two parallel and sharply contrasted characters and the directions their lives take, evoke a continuity of interest, an unconscious attempt on the reader's part to measure one against the other, and a probing and questioning of the values they individually represent. The point counter-point pattern of the plot thus rests heavily on the ever-shifting focus that oscillates between these two protagonists.

It is here that the critical view that rejects Gian as a possible protagonist needs to be examined. According to one view, Malgonkar's total rejection of Gandhism, in favour of the forgotten, obscure but glorious and heroic role of the other freedom fighters who fought the English with terror and violence, is symbolised in the character of Gian. Based on this gigantic misconception, Gian is seen as a totally negative character: he is unintelligent, cowardly, cunning, corrupt, mean and totally without conscience, "Whereever he went and whatever he did, every time and in all circumstances he betrayed his friends and took undue advantage of their friendship. Thoroughly corrupt and undependable, he cringed before his superiors and oppressed his subordinates."[8] This view is so obviously narrow, one-sided and erroneous that one need not even bother to refute it. As should be expected, at the other end of this simplistic, black-and-white view is the character of Debi who is seen as 'fearless, duty-conscious and patriotic', and truly heroic. This critic finds it ironical in the extreme that the good man should perish and the depraved one survive. A more balanced estimate is that of G.S. Amur who believes that Gian emerges, during the course of the novel, from the lower depths and redeems himself by endangering his life for the sake of love: "the Gian who survives is not the Gian who built his life on falsehood, but a morally regenerated individual."[9] Gian, who is not much given to articulating his inner, quite often confused and conflicting feelings, affirms his moral renewal when he travels into the riot-torn Panjab from the safety of Bombay, with the sole motive of rendering help to Sundari and her family and "to try and prove, if only to myself that there can be some good in the weakest of human beings."[10] What is generally not noticed is that Gian's comeback to decency begins earlier in Bombay where, tormented by a sense of guilt, he demands of Sundari a fuller life based on true love, and walks away from the sexual pleasures of a clandestine relationship; love for Sundari all this while having been a 'game', an excitement and an escape from the dull existence of a jilted wife. In fact, a matter of sustained interest in the novel is to watch the growth of Gian's character from an initially unformed, mixed-up youth of confused idealism to a middle stage that presents him as a murderer, informer and liar, struggling for sheer survival and finally to a responsible manhood in which he strives to retain a mere residue of self-respect and decency. In fact, Gian's return to help the Tekchand family—less of a heroic action than an act of fulfilment—and Tekchand's return from the convoy to be with his dead wife, are the only two clear assertions of positive values in a world of total chaos and destruction. Although presented as a counter-foil to the heroic Debi-dayal in the beginning, a running comparison between Gian and him becomes much less relevent in the later parts of the novel which show the complete dominance of characters by events: both Gian and Debi, regardless of their earlier states of mind, are submerged in the flood of violence that runs through the country. Their volitions, if at all they survive, particularly in the case of Debi, are left confused and weakened.

The second factor that lends unity and design to an otherwise shapeless plot is the unbroken recurrence of the patterns of betrayal and revenge. In fact, so forceful is the presence of this pattern that the reader is compelled to see the author's dominant view of society as base, destructive and brutal. Gian feels that he betrayed his brother Hari in not going to his help to fight Vishnu-dutt. In turn, he is betrayed by the servant Tukaram who is beaten and brutalized by the police to give false evidence. Even the bullocks Raja and Sarja, who were 'like children to Hari' are betrayed when they are sold to the Vaccine Institute where their bodies would be given razor-cuts and injected with small-pox serum. Shafi's betrayal of the Hindu members of Hanuman Club marks the break between the two communities and starts a violent and finatical war between them. Debi never renounces his bitter feeling that it was his own father who reported him to the police: consequently, the only two persons he hates most are Shafi and his father Tekchand. Gopal makes love to the society woman Malini within full view of his newly-wedded wife Sundari, thus causing one of the most unforgivable betrayals in the books. The second betrayal by Shafi takes place when under the pretext of friendship, he reports Debi's presence to the police to have him arrested. By then, there has been too much mutual distrust and hatred among the two communities. Towards the end, Tekchand's servants disappear, leaving his family defenceless and exposed to the violent mobs.

In the section depicting jail life in Andaman, this pattern of the human behaviour persists. Ghasita, the giant-sized criminal had murdered the man who had betrayed him to the authorities. Gian literally blows the whistle on Debi' for whom his secret admiration as a nationalist and a hero had remained undiminished. Greed and the instinct for survival impel Gial not only to cut open the throat of the dead Ghasita to rob the gold coins concealed in his 'khobri', but also to pose as Debi's friend to secure a job from his father Tekchand. Mulligan, the jail superintendent, who is a sort of father figure and in whose authority and presence the inmates have immense trust, abandons his post to save his own life. He even subverts the traditional Englishman's love for his dog, by leaving the bitch Delilah to its own fate. The Japanese who intitially raise a lot of hope and friendly feelings as the saviours of Andaman, belie these notions with greater cruelty and ruthlessness. Debi, who is chosen by the Japanese to go back to India as their agent 'betrays' them by hiding himself for the remaining period of the war. The English become guilty of the greatest betrayal of all when they run away at the Burma front, leaving behind thousands of Indian soldiers to fend for themselves. Their action belies their traditional colonial image as responsible guardians and 'ma-baap' (father-mother) of their subjects.

Betrayal which goes hand in hand with revenge becomes a complete motif with a number of 'revenge' incidents, largely arising as consequence to the acts of betrayal. Apart from the killings of Vishnu-dutt by Gian and of his betrayer by Ghasita, revenge becomes a strong motivating force in the lives of the characters, giving their actions a vital direction. Thus, Debi's ultra-nationalism is motivated by his desire to punish the English for the outrage on his mother. Shafi's militancy and his total commitment to the cause of a violent ouster of the English is brought on by the fact of his father's death at the historic Jallianwalla Bagh massacre and the humiliation inflicted by General Dyer's crawling order. Debi's strange revenge on Shafi, which prompts him to take away Shafi's woman Mumtaz is an uncharacteristic act on Debi's part and gives a melodramatic dimension to the story, particularly when it begins to unfold the deadly communal passions and massive violence. (It is not only the weakest link in the plot, it appears to be an obvious concession on the author's part to the popular taste) As if to lay down a rule for 'revenge' ethics, Ghasita tells Gian: "our god demands that anyone who betrays a confidence must be slain" (196). It is not difficult to see that Ghasita' code is hardly different from the one that operates in the civilized society.

Malgonkar thus controls his material, not so much through an arrangement of time and space but through the application of a certain pattern of human behaviour. It is rather inexplicable that anyone should regard it as one of the 'blemishes' of the novel.[11] This method gives proper shape and purpose to the plot inasmuch as it enables the author to project a rather stark and disturbing view of society. The social structure as we see it at the particular moment of history before independence, stands fragmented not only because of the intolerable colonial rule, it is riven by a thousand schisms of communal disharmony, greed and hatred. It is the scene of a violent society dangerously poised on the brink of disaster. The statue of Shiva, the lord of destruction, further cements this theme as it appears to preside over the incidents of violence and death. It beams across the sinister message 'A million shall die, a million!' when Gian first bows before it and sees in his imagination the bearded and malevolent face of the terrorist Shafi super-imposed on it. The same metallic statue of Shiva is the weapon with which Sundari, in self-defence, bashes Shafi's head into a pulp. This all-pervasive symbol, making its appearance at crucial moments in the plot, further strengthens its unity and cohesiveness.

It is often stated that the major theme of *A Bend in the Ganges* is the rejection of the Gandhian concept of non-violence. "It is, obviously, part of the novel's strategy to discredit non-violence and to demonstrate its ineffectiveness in the context of a life situation," thinks G.S. Amur.[12] The same critic goes on to argue that his brother's murder reveals to Gian the "un-reality of non-violence as a way of life" and that his revenge "proves to be an act of liberation and self-fulfilment." A rather inept version of this view goes like this: "*A Bend in the Ganges* shows Gandhi, the greatest opponent of the partition, the staunch champion of Hindu-Muslim unity and the true devotee of non-violence, *responsible* for the partition and violence in the wake of India's independence"[13] (emphasis added). Several other critics have too easily taken the view that *A Bend* has a 'thesis' which is to demonstrate the utter irrelevance of the Gandhian creed of non-violence in real life. This rather superficial evaluation of the novel unjustly discredits it and deviates the reader's attention from its depth, particularly from its central purpose of depicting individuals searching for meaning and values in a shattered, collapsing world.

Malgonkar himself is, to some extent, responsible for the mischief. The long Gandhi quotation in the beginning draws attention to the possibility of the book being an examination of the theme of non-violence: "Can true, voluntary non-violence come out of this seeming forced non-violence of the weak?" And the long speech by the young Nehru in chapter one declares, with philosophical clarification, non-violent war on the English: "But make no mistake: Our non-violence is the non-violence of the brave, arising not from cowardice but from courage. . ." Both these portions—Gandhi's quotation and Nehru's speech—are not only totally unnecessary and unrelated to the main plot, they invoke in the reader a false and erroneous expectation about the book being a testing ground for this thesis. Nowhere in the novel is there even a hint of a distinction between 'non-violence of the weak' and 'non-violence of the brave'. Moreover, Gandhi, and Nehru refer to the creed of non-violence as a political weapon: notice the dominant imagery in Nehru's speech which employs such words as 'soldiers', 'army of liberation', 'victory', 'weapons', 'war' etc. It is this undue emphasis on non-violence as a political strategy that gives a false start to the novel: its impact on the lives of the main characters is minimal and the public and the private levels of the meaning of non-violence remain largely unrelated.

Malgonkar, however, makes several attempts in the novel to connect this political theme with the individual, private lives. After the initial debate between Gian and Shafi in which the two positions are rather emphatically stated ("Non-violence is the philosophy of sheep, a creed for cowards"(18) and "No man has the right to raise his hand against another whatever the provocation" (19)), Gian is filled with remorse because he thinks that his cowardly non-violence prevented him from going to his brother's help. After such vague introspecton, Gian dismisses this subject from his mind for the rest of the narrative: so far as he is concerned, non-violence or violence as ways of life no longer occur in his reckoning as points of reference. It has been rightly observed that "non-violence for Gian was not a strongly felt creed but a temporary expedient."[14] Much later, this debate re-appears in Debi's life when, after two years of hiding at Silent Hills in eastern India, a very bewildered and mixed-up Debi contacts Basu, his old friend from their revolutionary days. When reacting to the large-scale communal strife, Debi remarks that "non-violence is perhaps the only answer" (290). Basu, however, retorts:

> Non-violence is merely a pious thought, a dream of the philosophers. I shudder to think what Gandhi will feel when he sees the holocaust that will engulf this country. He will die a thousand deaths. . . but will he ever recognize that mankind is not prepared for true non-violence—will never be prepared? No! No! He will go on living and preaching his dream (290-91).

Two more statements of Basu complete this academic discussion: "Non-violence is all very well if the other party too plays by the rules" (291) and "What is the future for a country nurtured on non-violence in a world of mounting violence?" (292). As stated earlier, this political aspect of the theme of non-violence is stated at a level that barely touches the lives of the individuals: it merely provides a 'thesis' that remains largely unrelated to the actual plot. Like Gian's, Debi's life too is no longer motivated at this stage by the philosophical considerations regarding the uses of violence or non-violence.

Actually, *A Bend* is an intimate study of communal and mob violence. The Author's Note in the beginning takes cognizance of this fact: "Only the violence in this story happens to be true; it came in the wake of freedom, to become a part of India's history. What *was achieved through non-violence,* brought with it one of the bloodiest upheavals of history" (emphasis added). And towards the end, the author describes the sober and conservative Tekchand say to himself: "Now he could see that as far as the people of India were concerned, Gandhi's message was merely a political expedient, that for the bulk of them, it had no deeper significance" (333).

Two points in this discussion are thus clearly conceded by Malgonkar: that non-violence indicates a state of perfection that may be difficult to achieve and that as a political instrument, non-violence has succeeded in bringing freedom to India. All this, at no stage, amounts to a rejection of the creed of non-violence. As against this, the violence that is described is self-destructive, evil and a direct nagation of life. How else, if not as a supreme irony, is one to understand the racial violence that sweeps the land like a tornado at the end, when men and women are scattered, without volition, like straws in the wind; and when Debi, the much proclaimed devotee of the creed of violence, is castrated and emasculated by a violent mob on the very day that the sun is rising for the first time on a free land. In this sense, *A Bend in the Ganges* is a powerful indictment of violence.

A Bend is Malgonkar's best achievement in terms of the tightness of style and intensity of expression although at times it suffers from raciness and thinness of material. The situations and places described have a ring of truth about them and the characters an unusual vitality. Although the reader is not given a close and intimate insight into the working of the characters' mind—a success in psychological probing that Malgonkar achieves in novels like *Combat of Shadows* and *The Devil's Wind*—the characters come alive in quick short jabs of description. To pick a few examples, Hari is "viceless, god-fearing, self-denying" (27), Aji is "tiny, wrinkled, rigid" (29), Shanker (Gian's father) was "unlettered, hot-headed, ineffectual" (40), Tomonaga is "obese, repulsive, deceptively soft" (69) and even the river was "secluded, opulent, forbidding" (12). Such pithiness, accompanied by a general economy of expression, imparts a starkness to the text and sharpens the reader's sense of apprehension.

Notes

1. G.S. Amur, *Manohar Malgonkar,* Arnold-Heinemann, New Delhi, p.9.
2. *Ibid.,* p.21.
3. *Ibid.,* p. 13.
4. R.S. Singh, *Indian Novel in English,* Arnold-Heinemann, New Delhi, p. 121.
5. *Combat of Shadows.* Orient paperback, p.55.
6. *Ibid.,* p. 56.
7. Amur, p. 91.
8. R.S. Singh, p. 129.
9. Amur, p. 108.
10. *A Bend in the Ganges,* Orient paperback, pp. 351-52. All other references to this novel are indicated by page numbers in parenthesis.
11. Amur, p. 121.
12. *Ibid.,* p. 104.
13. K.K. Sharma, "The 1947 Upheaval and the Indian-English Novel" in *Explorations in Modern Indo-English Fiction,* ed. R.K. Dhawan, Bahri Publications, New Delhi, 1982, p. 35.
14. Meenakshi Mukherjee, *The Twice Born Fiction,* Heinemann, New Delhi, p. 60.

BHABANI BHATTACHARYA: *Shadow from Ladakh*

Ramesh K. Srivastava

In range and appeal, in variety of characters and richness of plot, Bhabani Bhattacharya's *Shadow from Ladakh* towers above his other novels and is in fact the culmination of his genius. Having dealt with tradition and modernity in *Music for Mohini*, with hunger and poverty in *So Many Hungers!* and *He Who Rides a Tiger*, and superstition and magic cure in *A Goddess Named Gold*, Bhattacharya took up, for the first time, the subjects of defending the national frontiers in the wake of the Chinese aggression and of the country's dilemma in choosing its national policy between cottage and large-scale industries, and between Gandhian and western ways of life.

Published in 1966, *Shadow from Ladakh* deals with the Gandhian nation bracing itself to meet the challenge of the Chinese forces. The eruption of hostilities between China and India and the large-scale industries represented by Bhashkar and Lohapur endanger Gandhigram and Gandhian ideology of truth, non-violence, spinning wheel and cottage industries.

The novel won for its author the coveted Sahitya Akademi Award as it has depicted "a cross section of contemporary India during a period of tansition and rapid development and has reflected the intricate pattern of present-day life with a remarkable understanding and clarity."[1] However, the work has been criticized for being politically oriented and for having a contemporary situation for its setting. Even though the novel has a good plot, a fine style and a set of beautiful images which make it better than the rest, the question has often been raised, and not without some validity, whether "patriotic ardour contributed to the singling out of this particular book"[2] for the award. It is quite possible that the novel touched the bleeding hearts of its readers. The subject, however, raises two important points; first, should contemporary material be used in a literary work, and, second, should didacticism be permissible in a work of art?

C. Paul Verghese has been opposed to the use of the material of topical interest, considering that the novel would have been better in having a philosophical base instead of having too recent an event in fiction.[3] The reason given by him is that "an artist who turns recent events into fiction cannot easily succeed, for the unconscious mind requires much time to perform its wonder of transmuting incident into art."[4] Bhattacharya is not opposed to the idea of using a contemporary event in the novel; nor does he accept the view that the contemporary reality, because of its intense emotional appeal and by becoming outdated with the passage of time, prevents an author from being dispassionate, detached and universal, thereby allowing the work to be biased. Bhattacharya uses a contemporary event—the Chinese aggression of 1962—to form the background of this novel. Favouring the use of contemporary material, he fears that if sometime is allowed to lapse, as advised by others, the contemporary reality might be blurred and its sharpness lost whereas it should be like a powerful wave, a volcanic eruption, demanding a spontaneous creative outlet. There is nothing wrong if a novelist is concerned with the current hour or moment "if it is meaningful for him, if it moves him sufficiently into emotional response."[5] The event of the Chinese agression must have moved him sufficiently, but might it also not have made him partial and biased?

Of course, the whole novel is not about the Chinese aggression but it does portray the dilemma most Indians faced then and discussed at several places; should it abandon the path of peaceful co-existence and arm itself to teeth? Should it abandon the path of Gandhi and his non-violence to be able to show an eye for the invader's eye and tooth for the traitor's tooth? Gandhi's truth and non-violence which could stand well against the British fell ineffectively before the Chinese aggression. The Chinese invasion was virtually the death-knell of Gandhian values. During the traumatic experience the nation had, people in their suppressed tone blamed Gandhiji for incapacitating the nation to fight by advocating non-violence as they blamed Nehru for not visualizing the

Chinese designs in spite of many warnings to the contrary after their annexation of Tibet.

It is here that Bhattacharya's synthesis of the two comes in the picture. For him Mahatma Gandhi's advocacy of non-violence and cottage industries was both a political and economic weapon to transform the country into Ramrajya where each village would be self-sufficient and would not have to look to the city for guidance and help. Nehru wanted to place the country on the world map of technical, scientific and industrial advancement. The question became urgent after our humiliating defeat in confrontation with the Chinese and merited a literary representation.

Gandhigram and Steel town are not simply two localities but concrete symbols of Gandhian and Nehruite ways of life—one believing in simple living and cottage industries whereas the other in Western ways of life and industrialisation, Having a geographical area of four square miles, Gandhigram is an ideal model of rural order based on equality and economic self-sufficiency. Planned on the model of Gandhi's Sevagram, consisting of about two hundred mud-houses, the village has people living a simple life, putting on conchshell wristlets and coloured glasses. Men and women produce handloom cloth, cartwheel rims, pots and pans, jaggery and paper. Here decisions are taken not by any court or a magistrate but by the Council of Five.

But what is important here is not the physical shape of the village or what the occupations of the people are but what Bires calls "the Idea." However, the idea *alone* is not enough. If it were, the idea and the people along with their belongings could have been shifted from Gandhigram, as Bhashkar had suggested, for the expansion of Steeltown. It is also the sense of place, as Satyajit feels, which keeps the people so deeply rooted to the soil, that they cannot be uprooted and replanted elsewhere. Satyajit says, "The challenge isn't just between Gandhigram and Steeltown. It is between two contrary thoughts, two contrary ways of life. The spinning wheel set against the Steelmill!"[6]

Steeltown, on the other hand, symbolizes economic progress with the help of machine tools, tractors, big industrial plants and locomotives. It believes in mass production and rapid industrialization. But whereas amity characterizes Gandhigram, Steeltown seems to have a repressive nature, fattens upon rural environment and values, replaces simplicity by sophistication, ease with speed, manual by mechanical labour, and primitive devices by endless gadgets. Bhashkar's reasoning in favour of steel is: "The babies would not eat steel. But steel was the spine of the economy. Steel was food and clothing and dwelling. Steel was culture and art and ritual. And steel was soon to be the honour of the people, the shield of their freedom" (p. 37).

From Gandhigram and Steeltown, Bhattacharya extends the significance of these two symbols to the international level in which they become related to India and China: Two neighbours again, Gandhigram and Steeltown"

(p. 73). Subsequent references such as "expansion", "annexing of territory" and contrary "outlook" of Steeltown make it almost clear that Gandhigram with its emphasis on spiritual life is India in miniature and Steeltown the epitome of the aggressive China. A peaceful village, Gandhigram, is disturbed by the fast-expanding steeltown. A peaceful country, India, gradually awakening after centuries of slavery and sleep, crawling in its medieval, non-technological life, is jolted now out of its complacency by the brutal force of the Chinese aggression. In the process what is lost is not only thousands of miles of India's territory but the very concept of non-violence and peaceful co-existence. It was the victory of Steeltown over Gandhigram in the international conflict. The language Bhashkar uses echoes the language of the Chinese Premier:

> Expansion. We have to take Gandhigram in our stride. Our natural line of advance, from the technical point of view. It doesn't make sense to leave out this site and turn in some other direction. But there's a second reason why Gandhigram must be annexed. Its whole outlook is contrary to ours. It is what we've got to fight all over India (p. 130).

Bhattacharya gives the background of the winter of 1959. The Chinese took possession of thousands of miles of Indian territory in order to have an easy route between Sinkiang and western Tibet at a time when both the countries had the friendliest of relations. Then it launched an attack in 1962, disregarding this friendship, violating the principles of Panchsheel— five principles—laid down in the Conference of Asian countries at Bandung, which included among others, mutual respect for territorial integrity. At this stage, India was virtually forced to get ready for the worst. In order to defend its borders, it had to leave the path of non-violence and to resort to the manufacture of arms. Bhashkar who used various persuasive tactics over Satyajit in vain now gleefully thinks: "Peking had settled the fate of Gandhigram and it was too late for the slow way of persuasion" (p. 177).

On another level, Gandhigram and Steeltown can be associated with past, present and future. Gandhigram symbolizes the past and Steeltown the present. Associated with primitive simplicity, Gandhigram is Adam's paradise before his fall—an archetypal haven in its opposition to scientific and technological knowledge, believing in primitive life as opposed to modernity. An apple of knowledge brought Adam's paradise down, and "the electric switch, that small button, may eventually bring about the end of Gandhigram" (p. 142). Steeltown belongs to the present as the country needs iron and steel for construction activities. But the physical requirements of a country, its construction activities, symbolized by Steeltown, cannot go on forever. When its uses are exhausted, its surfeit becomes tiring, then comes a desire for primitive simplicity, and for spiritualism represented by Gandhigram and hence it symbolizes future. Spiritualism then will replace materialism. This is what Satyajit says, "When the material benefits of production have been fully attained, Steeltown, decrepit and soulless, will have to seek new moorings. Then it will be Gandhigram's turn to come forward" (p. 156).

Since at some stage or other, Gandhigram and Steeltown are necessary, the country cannot have one at the cost of the other. That would be like having present without past or future without present. Steeltown and Gandhigram are like body and soul. One cannot exist without the other. This is what Mrs. Mehra means when she poohpoohs the plea to return to Gandhigram. "Return? There can be no return. Feed your spirit while you feed your body, or else the spirit will not survive. You can't do this one by one" (p. 200).

Believing in the integration of the two, Bhattacharya gives the example of Shantiniketan which is the concretization of Tagore's firm belief: "Integration—that was the poet's lifelong quest: integration of the simple and the sophisticated; the ancient and the modern; city and village; East and West" (p. 215). In the end, Bhashkar realizes the significance of Gandhigram and adopts the path of reconciliation instead of confrontation.

For Chandrasekharan, it is not a co-existence of different ideologies but a reconciliation and an apt plea of Bhattacharya for adopting "the way of integration and synthesis"[7] of Gandhigram and Steeltown, the kind of reconciliation in which "each meets the other halfway

Shadow from Ladakh

and each surrenders and makes a sacrifice to make the synthesis possible."⁸ This is seen in the construction of the Meadow House— a meeting place of Gandhigram and Steeltown—for encouraging cultural activities, including western dances, as also for providing a meeting ground of different sexes. The same principle of co-existence, compromise and readjustment is seen in the marriage of Sumita and Bhashkar, in Satyajit's new resolve to come down from the Olympian heights of asceticism in order to live a natural, human life, and, finally, in Bhashkar's resolve to expand the Steeltown but in another direction, allowing Gandhigram to "live as long as it has vitality within" (p. 355). This is the real synthesis of ideologies of Gandhi and Nehru which is what the country has today.

Another theme treated in the novel is that of youth and age. In the country of ancient civilization—of saints, gurus and acharyas, the age rather than the youth, the father rather than the son, the teacher rather than the taught, and the guru rather than the disciple have always been the guiding spirits behind the activities of the young people, particularly when complex questions and puzzling options were involved. In the modern times with the growth of education and scientific advancement, the youth has left the age behind, snatching the reign of progress and administration. The attitude of the old people, however, still remains unchanged. Bhattacharya, knowing the need of the hour, and aware of the fact that the well being of the country lies in the changed values, treats this theme very skilfully.

Bhattacharya poses this problem through Rangaswamy who tells Bhashkar that the latter is young and that it is rare for a person of his age to hold a high post in the country, even though such a thing is quite normal in the United States which is an advanced country and where merit counts. Bhashkar replies rather scornfully, "In this country youth stands nowhere. Age alone counts. One becomes wiser under the sheer weight of one's years" (p. 59). Two reasons pointed out by Rangaswamy against the youth are: one, that they are sentimental, and the other, that they are impulsive, either of which the country cannot afford to put up with at this stage. Bhattacharya knows the potentialities of the youth as also their weaknesses and points them out through the portrayal of four Chinese children—daughters of a Chinese shoe-maker—who, after their father has been arrested, are given asylum in Bhashkar's house. Bhashkar notices their sincerity and devotion, their innocence and purity He realizes that the younger generation can create wonders, bring miracles, and build bridges of international understanding, the kind they had built between themselves and Bhashkar. As they brought transformation in Bhashkar, they can do so in China:

> Slender and small, they are fighting the battle of humanity which their vast powerful country had already lost. Their victory over a minute area of the spirit had to make up for all the inner poverty that the leaders of their ancient race were showing today. (p. 257)

While the older generation has become strongly biased, both in India and in China, the younger generation remains untouched. The school children in India treat the Chinese children as if they were of their own country without any sense of discrimination or coldness. The Chinese children develop so much attachment with India and Bhashkar that they feel anguished at the thought of leaving them and promise to work on bringing about an understanding between the two countries.

This brings us to the second question, raised in the beginning of this paper, with regard to didacticism in the novel. Bhattacharya has been opposed to the idea of art for art's sake and advocates art for life's sake. His art being purposive, the novel in his hand becomes an instrument to bring about an awareness of social reality. Values in art must follow values in life, for the artist is a human being among human beings. Literature which steers clear of the vast humanscape is devoid of universal truth. Dealing with truths leads the artist inevitably to deal with ethical values, though a fine balance has to be struck to save an artist from degenerating into a moralist. "Art must preach," says Bhattacharya, "but unobtrusively, by the vivid interpretation of life. Art must preach, but not by virtue of its being a vehicle of truth. If it is propaganda, there is no need to eschew the word."[9] Keeping Bhattacharya's above views in mind, one can call *Shadow from Ladakh* not a didactic work or a novel of propaganda but the concrete transformation of Gandhian and Western values into a work of art.

The novel has a great variety of characters but the protagonists lack depth and fineness.[10] In characterization, too, Bhattacharya uses the devices of parallelism and contrast which he had in the portrayal of Gandhigram and Steeltown, youth and age. Satyajit is compared and constrasted with Bhashkar and Bireswar, and Sumita with Jhanak and Rupa. Satyajit believes in Gandhian ideas; Bhashkar in those of Nehru. Satyajit chooses morality and spiritualism; Bhashkar materialism. The former believes in simple, ascetic life; the latter in Western ways of living. Even Bireswar is close to Bhashkar and is opposed to Satyajit's asceticism which is at the cost of his wife's happiness. Believing in the Gandhian principles of castelessness for which he is prepared to lay down his life, he discards **his surname** indicative of his caste affiliations. He uses homespun cloth for a bedspread, tries to adopt the idea of brahmacharya in thought and action, and of non-violence and simple living. For him, mechanization is evil only if it made people idle; otherwise he approves of it. For Bhashkar, Satyajit is not the leader of Gandhigram; "*He* is Gandhigram. Without his guidance the structure of ideas he's been building will topple like a thing of sand", (p.131). As if to bring two of Gandhi's main characterstics of truth and non-violence, his name suggests victory of truth, while his work *The Conquest of Violence* advocates non-violence. In the face of the Chinese aggression when most people believed that only violence could succeed against violence, he wishes to convert the hearts of the Chinese by organizing a peace march to Ladakh.

Shadow from Ladakh

In Bhashkar, Steeltown has its own exponent. Living in "the massive concrete-and-glass structure named steelhouse" (p. 34), he is the Chief Engineer of Lohapur Steel Company. He dresses in the Western way, is fond of wine and women, and believes that economic progress is possible only with mass production. If a few hands become idle or if a village has to be uprooted, it does not matter for him. Though the aims of Satyajit and Bhashkar are common, the preservation of national Independence and the removal of poverty, their means are quite different. Unlike Satyajit for whom means are as important as ends and who says "You can never attain good through evil" (p. 32), Bhashkar, by his modern ways of living believes that "ends justify means" (p. 32). Satyajit may be indispensable for Gandhigram, but Bhashkar is not for Steeltown. Satyajit's place can be taken by none, but when Bhashkar falls ill, nothing happens: "In the world of machines every individual is expendable" (p. 147).

Viewed from an artistic angle, Bhattacharya's characters, in this novel, seem to be human-shaped robots, going along pre-determined tracks. Some of them, like Satyajit and Bhashkar, are allegorical figures, carrying their identity cards, their set roles assigned by the author. Bhattacharya himself believed: "Characters have a volition of their own. They refuse to be puppets moved by invisible strings. They challenge the intention of their creator as they give shape and meaning to their own lives."[1] However, this does not seem to be so in this novel. Satyajit and Bhashkar, though good studies in contrast, appear not so much creatures of flesh and blood as the animated figures of Gandhi and Nehru. Principles rather than persons, ideas rather than feelings mark their characterization. Satyajit, like Moorthy in Raja Rao's *Kanthapura*, is an embodiment of Gandhian principles of truth, non-violence, renunciation, sacrifice, moral force and compassion, but unlike Moorthy, devoid of a convincing and throbbing human existence. For Moorthy is a wonderful fusion of principles and feelings whereas the personalities of Satyajit and Bhashkar turn pale and anaemic, even skeletal, before their glaring principles. Satyajit, carrying the high ideals of the Mahatma, does not appear to be at ease with his freight. It makes him self-conscious, somewhat rigid, as if the principles were not a part of him but he and his principles were two entities yoked together. It is this self-consciousness which does not let him live a full-blooded life. When he yields to his instincts, he chastises his body. He even makes his wife Suruchi unhappy because of his rigid adherence to asceticism.

For minor characters, too, Bhattacharya uses the devices of parallelism and contrast. Sumita, treading on the path of Satyajit, becomes ascetic and wants to dedicate her life for a cause, suppressing her instictive drives. For Fisher, Sumita is a "flat" and "one-dimensional"[12] character in her decision to dedicate herself to her father, ignoring her own life. Raizada calls her Satyajit's *"alter ego"*.[13] In contrast, Suruchi, while showing her regard to her husband's principles, knows a woman's needs and the

Shadow from Ladakh

fact that what she has suffered should not be suffered by her daughter Sumita and hence encourages her advances towards Bhashkar. Jhanak, too, can be contrasted with Sumita. While Sumita suppresses her natural self, Jhanak has "a woman's primal urges to be nothing but a woman" (p. 274) and is a "bright cactus bloom on the village earth" (p. 268). She revolts against rural traditions and defies Gandhigram by going for a movie with a youth. For people of the village, her act is an attempt to destroy Gandhigram from within as Bhashkar was doing from without. Rupa is beautiful, warm and loving. She, too, like Bhashkar, is westernized. For Fisher, Rupa is "Eve rather than Mary, seductress rather than mother."[14] Sumita and Rupa, like Satyajit and Bhashkar, have contrasting natures. Bhattacharya writes: "Sumita and Rupa. The Spinning Wheel and the turbine. India of epic age and India-to-be" (p. 122).

Since the subject matter of the novel is of national importance, deserving to be treated on an epic level, the language in *Shadow from Ladakh* becomes dignified. Here Bhattacharya's style[15] reaches, like the scene of the action of the novel, the Himalayan heights. Distinct signs of maturity appear from the very first page. Gone are the self-conscious steps behind which traces of effort were visible in his earlier novels, such as, *Music for Mohini* and *So Many Hungers*! In this novel, the style moves naturally and with dignity yet with a regal bearing as if Bhattacharya were a born prince, and not an actor playing the role of one. The style is charged with deep emotions, like the iron, expertly tampered. Matching with the heights of action of the novel, the style gains dignity; it moves, as it were, with the beat of drums, flies and soars with visionary ideas, pauses and falters in uncertain situations, and occasionally tickles and teases by its sharp and agile movements. It rings with political, scientific, military terms and with slogans, such as, *Hindi-Chini Bhai bhai,* which still reverberate in our memory.

There are occasions when the style becomes reflective and fresh, moving rhythmically, carrying the emotional burden in an appropriate language:

> That bullet had hit more than mere flesh—it had pierced a banner: the banner of love and non-violence that had been the undoing of a proud empire. But a frail old man, bespectacled and with a sharply pointed beard, now arose with dramatic suddenness, picked up the fallen emblem of love, and continued the work of spiritual reconstruction. He walked the country with a few chosen followers, walked thousands of miles, and, as insatiable as the Buddha twenty-five hundred years before, he bade the people renounce, renounce, renounce whatever they could, renounce all. He bade the landed gentry give a portion of their earth to the landless. He, nonviolent neo-Marx, sought a redistribution of wealth through the instrument of the heart, the inherent goodness of the human spirit! (p. 13).

His sentences, in this novel, are no longer simple but draped in festive garment, with silver or gold laces of similes, metaphors and pictorial phrases to illustrate and to embellish his prose, as if the subject matter demanded it. The flaring of lightning is compared to "a writhing fire snake" (p. 145); the voice of Peking to "ceaseless rain" (p. 168); Mrs Mehra without her husband to "a clock with dial but no works inside; or the works intact but no dial" (p. 202); and the pouring Chinese appear "like a torrent gone mad" (p. 245).

As opposed to the narrative or descriptive prose which is regal and dignified, Bhattacharya's dialogues in this novel seem bookish and theoretical. They seem to be of men and women devoid of their individualities. The heavy intellectualized dialogues, deprived of their natural flow, tailored to the dominant philosophy in the novel, make the characters appear like robots with their heads swollen and working. They rarely talk of mundane things but of high principles, ideas, ideals, plans. Here the dialogues are not of characters who are hungry for bread or for money, but for Steelhouse expansion, or for retaining Gandhigram. It appears that Bhattacharya was a pedestrian in *So Many Hungers!* and *He Who Rides a Tiger*, talking with people, listening to their pathetic cries, recording the very words uttered by them in their hours of strength and weakness, but here he soars in the sky, with some of his characters like Satyajit, Bhashkar, Suruchi and Sumita trailing closely behind, and they talk so big about principles and projects that Bhattacharya forgets the average human being crawling on earth too insignificant to have his passions and feelings recorded in natural dialogues.

The final impression of *Shadow from Ladakh* is like that of a beautiful and ornamented girl paraded on the stage as a princess, with an assigned role and a set of given dialogues, who holds the audience captivated, but as the certain is drawn, the audience murmurs, "How fantastic but how unlike us!"

Notes

1. Quoted by Dorothy Blair Shimer, *Bhabani Bhattacharya* (New York: Twayne-Publishers, 1975) p. 19.
2. Dorothy Blair Shimer, p. 68.
3. C. Paul Verghese, "Indian English and Man in Indo-Anglian Fiction," *Indian Literature*, 13, No. 1 (March 1970), 15.
4. C. Paul Verghese, "The Problem of the Indian Novelist in English," *The Banasthali Patrika*, No. 12 (January, 1969), p. 87.
5. Iqbal Bakhtiar (ed.), *The Novel in Modern India* (Bombay: P.E.N. All-India Centre, 1964), p. 47.
6. Bhabani Bhattacharya, *Shadow from Ladakh* (Delhi: Orient Paperbacks, 1966), p. 342. Subsequent references to this novel will be to the same edition.
7. K.R. Chandrasekharan, *Bhabani Bhattacharya* (New Delhi: Arnold-Heinemann Publishers, 1974) p. 124.
8. *Ibid.*, p. 125.
9. Bhabani Bhattacharya, "Literature and Social Reality", *The Aryan Path*, Vol. XXVI, No. 9 (Sept. 1955). 395.

10. For a detailed discussion of Bhattacharya's characterization, see "Introduction" in my edited book *Perspectives on Bhabani Bhattacharya* (Ghaziabad: Vimal Prakashan, 1982), pp. xxxiv-xl.
11. Bhabani Bhattacharya in *Contemporary Novelists in the English Language* (New York: St. Martin's Press, 1972) p. 38.
12. Marlene Fisher. "The Women in Bhattacharya's Novels," *World Literature Written in English*, Vol. XI, No. 1, April 1972, 104-105.
13. Harish Raizada, "Fiction as Allegory: Novels of Bhabani Bhattacharya," in *Perspectives on Bhabani Bhattacharya*, p. 95.
14. Marlene Fisher, p. 105.
15. For a detailed discussion of Bhattacharya's style, see my article "Bhattacharya's Prose Style" in *Perspectives on Bhabani Bhattacharya*, pp. 111-126.

ARUN JOSHI: *The Foreigner*

Devinder Mohan

In *The Foreigner,* Arun Joshi presents an image of Death by making it a fictional object as well as a manifestation of the presence which manipulates the event and the characters. The context of this presence offers possibilities of man's survival in contemporary conditions of ethno-history; man, for the first time, begins to exist against its closed abstractions acknowledging his inner madness.[1] Its limits are recognized in the territorial space of history which maintains *itself* in the life of its community (Babu Khemka and June Blyth) subjected to it, rather than to man, for its own perpetuation. In spite of its presence, however, man exists (Sindhi Oberoi) with all his corporeality and madness as necessary conditions for his existentiality.

Within the possibilities of the fictional craft of human consciousness, Arun Joshi succeeds in making this image articulate by situating the protagonist, Sindi Oberoi, as both the object and metaphor of man's unnamable madness, a kind of signifier who stays unformed beneath the difference of man's corporeality, his economical needs and his urgency to express, all of which, enable him to maintain what Michel Foucault calls 'finitude'.[2]

Sindi Oberoi is not the product of contemporary ethnology of the adjacent cultures of the world; rather their ethnology itself becomes the object for unformed subjectivity. This ethnology has lost its episteme and possibilities of transcendence. It has lost its dimension in which "its relations occur with each of the three great positivities (life need, labour and language)", [2a] and all that is left is a madness which eludes all signification.

Sindi Oberoi is also the signifier of the author's structural point of view.[3] We recognize the madness in its present form through his position with other characters. In recognising these characters as psychological projections (in many ways, artistic functions) of death, the reader needs to stay adjacent to Sindi Oberoi since he maintains a continued sense of adjacency with death as the evolving signifier of madness in the life of June Blyth and Babu Khemka; it spreads itself in the cultural world to which they belong. Babu Khemka and June Blyth omit the presence of death in escaping their own needs since they are only concerned to fulfil somebody else's need. They think that they can find their salvation outside their own physiology, outside the verbal space across their surrounding madness in human life. Before they begin to leap forward, their space breaks short of self-interrogating awareness.

The Foreigner, like the rest of Joshi's novels, suffers at the hands of critics from abstract generalisations of themes which have no bearing on the form of the novel, a fiction of presentational immediacy of consciousness obssessed with death and madness. They talk about alienation, self-delusion,[4] mode of anxiety[5] detachment solution, the interior "I" and the reflective insiders.[6] These themes, however, echo individually and in mixed mode, the forming of the image with the spiral progress of subjectivity, not so much as an action against the system of the historical event (Babu Khemka's death), but as a kind of dispersion of madness against the consuming waves of death. In many ways, Sindi Oberoi becomes a watchword of madness, the twin counterpart of death[7], going hand in hand and in equal pace along the motion of mutual dispersions. His presence is a metonymic extension of the presence of death whereas other characters manifest their transitory subjectivity. Shiela's presence provides the necessary difference, for the developing form of the image of death within the feel of immersion in madness.

Death as a devastating form of degradation of man's past, his history, his language, flashes across the opening scene of the novel. June Blyth and Babu Khemka are suggested as its glimmering exteriority to the reader. In this context, they become its discontinuous 'signs' within their own imagined possibilities in reaching for a sense of meaning in life. In these possibilities, each of their lives does not open up more than a darkening cry, of a space too inadequate for their voices to be heard against the silent spectacle of madness. Death as event is transformed as an aesthetic sign of its "presentational presence"[8], a kind of its own "discursive dispersion"[9] in a complex network of all the characters of the novel. They maintain their diversity as distinct signifying forms against the nagging absence of a sense of fulfillment, a sense, indeed, of a lament for signification across the space of human life. Consider the opening scene:

> They uncovered his face and I turned away in spite of myself.
> "Will you please look at the body, Mr. Oberoi"?
> A dark bottomless hole gaped in place of the right eye. The sensual upper lip was gone, leaving behind a horrible grin that showed no sign of ending.
> "Should I remove the sheet?"
> "No," I said quickly. "Don't bother".
> "Do you know him?"
> "Yes. Babu Khemka. Babu Rao Khemka."
> "Student?"
> "Yes."
> "Which department?" The man spoke tonelessly, his face without expression.
> "Engineering," I said.
> "Do you know where he lives?" the man asked. He took out a pack of Viceroys. The ad said Viceroy men are men of the world.
> I was suddenly tired.
> "No," I said, letting out a sigh in little jerks, "Somewhere on Pine Street." It was surprising that I had never been to Babu's place.
> "Put him back," the man said to the attendant.
> "What happened?" I asked because I thought it was expected of me.

"Car wreck on Mass Turnpike. Rolled off a bridge." . . . . "Do you know a girl named June Blyth?" the man asked. "Yes." I said, and waited for the worst.

He shrugged, "We found her picture in his wallet. Will you tell her?"

Yes, I'll tell her", I said, relieved.[10]

As the scene germinates in the mind of the reader, the attendants of the dead body flicker in the madness that caused the event like faces groping in darkness. The words of the opening sentence raise the curtain to uncover the terror of silence at the extremity of death feeding on the resonance of life, labour and language.[11] This resonance begins with the fictional dialogue between the protagonist speaking with smaller words (myself) and the reader, through dispersion of the event in mental flash-blacks. The body becomes a discontinuous sign of death to evolve a kind of dialogue amongst its attendants through the images of death in their lives and in the life of the victim. The victim was a student from India for an engineering degree in an American university and the inquiring man is a 'Man of the world', being of the American world, taking out a Viceroy pack. Babu Khemka is required by his parents to get a foreign degree in order to perpetuate the family tradition of cultural facade. Since this wish is not his own wish, it is not his need (he is never free enough to interrogate his life in terms of his own needs). Ironically, however, he is perpetuated to fill in the needs of others, first of his own parents, then, perhaps, of the world surrounding him in America. The man of the world in America suggests the absurdity of human situation caught in the cultural facade. Both of them hasten to the extremity of the death image even in their life styles; both of them blend with its intrinsic subjectivity carrried on in the dialogue between the protagonist and the reader. Sindi's agreeing that he will break the news about Babu's death to June Blyth, initiates the dispersion of the event in her life too. "She carried death with her", says Sindi Oberoi, the spectator-participant protagonist. And then!

> "Babu is dead," I said after a while. There seemed to be no other way of saying it. I don't think she really believed it for a minute. I was right; she didn't realize we had killed a man. I hated myself, but for her I felt only pity.
>
> "Babu is dead, June" I said again. "He had an accident on Mass Turnpike."(6)

Death has entered in her consciousness and in the cultural consciousness of Boston, city of 'sick hurry and divided aims' (to use Matthew Arnold's phrase). She chooses to fill in Babu's need, somebody outside her own culture, already emaciated like her, escaping his own need and his family's. Then she turns to somebody who is inside both the cultures, but outside their facades.

> "What shall I do, Sindi? What shall I do?" My poor, poor, girl, I thought. I rubbed her back to ease her crying. I said, "There is nothing you can do, my poor love. It is all over. I should have known better."(6)

Sindi admits the event as a fact of life with all its horror and guilt, a fact signifying the absence of life, labour and language.

In the following chapters, the glimmers of life show up in death's darkness, in Sindi Oberoi's witnessing gaze. As indicated earlier, he comes across as the structural principal of the aesthetic distance, both inside and outside the action, and thus, in many ways, an artistic discourse of death viberating in contemporary ethnology of human civilization. What is missing is a sense circulation of eternality within the system of human physiology, of the cultural life of Delhi and Boston. What is in circulation is the episteme of madness which has not yet caught up with the "language of finitude" of "man assignable in his corporeal, labouring and speaking existence."[12] This episteme is at the parodoxical point of stillness and motion.[13] When Sindi comes back to India to break the news to Khemka's family (carrying Babu's madness, June's madness and their death) there is a critical "gaze"[14] at the ruins of Indian civilization, as there is also at American civilization when he visits June's mother.

This was no doubt India's affluent society. Plush carpets, low streamlined divans, invisible lighting, bell buttons in every corner, and sculpture. That is where Babu must have played as a child. The rich Persian carpets, those sculpture-ridden walls must have concocted the innocence that destroyed him and very nearly buried me.(9)

What is dispersed in this gaze is that Babu Khemka had all those comforts which made him too protective to make contact with his physiology, with his economic needs, outside the orbit of his family and its needs, outside indeed the utilitarian language of the life surrounding him.

But this gaze is almost blinded when Sindi encounters Sheila in the Khemka family. There is a mythical shift of Indianism, a shift from the material luxuries trapping the human soul for their own abstracting darkness, to some kind of divine presence which is not allowed to have its own language in the forms of Khemka's Indian culture:

> We sat at the edge of an enormous rosewood dining table laid with expensive cut-glass and polished silver. Sheila sat at the head of the table. Behind her, in an alcove, stood a bronze figure of dancing Shiva. For a moment, just one brief moment, I was struck by the intense beauty of the divine dancer. America, India, Egypt, all mingled behind him in aeons of increasing

rhythm. The dance went on unheeding, and yet comprehending all, (11).

The bronze figure of the dancing Shiva is only a decorative piece, like the rosewood dining table, to fill the Khemkas' material needs. This world of appearances is all that the Khemkas cared for, worked for, even committed crimes for. But against the added glitter that money could procure, stood the authetic presence of Shiva, consuming it, almost mocking it. Shiela, below this figure, passive unadorned, uncared, being a woman, being part of somebody else's home in the future has no communication with the Khemkas. Like Shiva, she is a foreigner to Khemka's Indianism. Sheila's presence, which merges with Shiva's dance, although pushed too far back, is almost buried down beneath the utilitarian life style. She refers to Joshi's voice of fictional authority, mute unattainable, within the forms of madness. This voice does not make any calls either; it would stay in the background to be discovered, desired and 'worked for. But it remains at the edge of even Sindi's gaze, at Khemka's gradually heading for death and at his own world of madness.

> . . .the chasm of a living world prevailed. I had a feeling that I was watching her from the edge of the world just where Death's Kingdom began. (14).

The Foreigner

Shiela stays at this edge, calm like an untouchable sadness, in spite of the world of servitude, until the end of the novel, when her father goes to jail on account of tax evasion and Sindi still continuing to gaze at life (Shiela) and death (Khemkas, their Indianism).

Babu Khemka is a foreigner to the system of the Khemkas, being not much of Khemka material to meet their need, and therefore his own. Shiela too is a foreigner to that system, since she outlives this system in Babu Khemka beyond a point in time when it crumbles. Sindhi Oberoi is a foreigner too, to this system, as well as to the American system, since he stays at the extremity where both of them become brittle, and break their ground:

> You had a clear-cut system of morality, a caste system that laid down all you had to do. You had a God; You had roots in the soil you lived upon. Look at me. I have no roots. I have no system of morality. What does it mean to me if you call me an immoral man? I have no reason to be one thing rather than another. You ask me why I am not ambitious; well, I have no reason to be. Come to think of it I don't even have a reason to live. (138-39).

And Shiela is on the other extremity, 'a man high flame' high up, on the mountain, in which Bilasia's (*The Strange Case of Billy Biswas*) and Anuradha's (*The Last Labyrinth*) language of intricate human relationships is purged and consummated, for its own presence. Sindi and Shiela gaze at each other from their own extremities of death and life, of madness and divinity, of history and its rupture, for the priestly function of languate. Language keeps polarising, mediating, sustaining these stubborn extremities.

But Sindi Oberoi would not accept the other extremity. He carries his burden and his world's, his own guilt and the world's, his own madness and the world's, since he is surrounded by people groaning under this burden; he must be that act of burden himself, its subjectivity, its episteme, its word, regardless of the fact that June Blyth too perishes like Babu. Like her own culture, she has no roots. She is lonely but she would not accept this as her burden, a fact of life with all its necessary terror. She would survive if she floats like rootless people such as Karl.

> Every time I have an affair, I promise myself it will be the last one. But the same thing happens over and over again. Some lonely wretch takes me home and pulls me on top of her. I feel her lusty naked body and in a moment all my vows are forgotten. I go through the motions and I hear her moan with pleasure under me. And I know it is I, Karl, who is giving her this pleasure. (60).

Karl refers to a static signifier of American culture, its facade within which its participants can only float. June's need is love, marriage, children, but isn't this of her ancestry, of her nostalgic recial past and not of the life surrounding her during the historical moment which confronts her? When she poses this question to Sindi, he confronts this moment, but she is not prepared for that:

> "Isn't it worth while to love somebody, make somebody happy, bring up children who contribute to society?"
>
> "And then what? Death wipes out everything, for most of us anyway. All that is left is a big mocking zero." And besides. I wanted to add. I was worried about my own contribution, leaving aside that of my children, (107).

And again:

> But in my world there are no statues of liberty. In my world many things are inevitable, and what's more, most of them are sad and painful. I can't come to your world. I have no escape, June. I just have no escape. (121)

There is then, no verbal space between them to come home to each other without each other's burden, and thus make language without destroying themselves as signifiers of their own individualities, however empty, lonely, and fearful they might seem. But she comes to him pregnant with Babu Khemka's child who dies of an accident, unable to make a human space for herself first. Escaping her own space as a person in society, she dies of abortion. Both Babu and June die, 'gazing' at death in their life times, living in foreign dreams aspiring beyond what historical condition can offer. Each of them marks the dispersions of their lives in terms of their death.

While 'glazing' at their death through its dispersion within the historical condition, Sindi recognises:

My foreignness lay within me and I couldn't leave myself behind wherever I went. . . Now I suppose I existed only for dying; so far as I knew everybody else did the same thing. It was sad, nonetheless. (61).

Sindi Oberoi is not T.S. Eliot's Prufrock,[15] since the episteme is essentially of madness. In many ways, his consciousness reverberates with psychological projections of death, in the horror of loneliness in human life, inspite of the material prosperity of American life and the corrupt capitalism of India of which the Khemka family becomes its ultimate victim. In the synchronic correlation of the complexity of both the cultures which Sindhi embodies, there is a persistent condition of madness for which the community of the non-verbal (the presence of Dance of Shiva signified in Shiela) does not get space for realizing man's essential finitude.

Arun Joshi reveals the world of madness as the grim possibility of realising its edge even with self-interrogation, which encloses for our side of it, nudity, sexuality, madness and death:

When this language emerges in all its nudity, yet at the same time eludes all signification as if it were a vast and empty despotic system, when Desire reigns in the wild state, as if the rigour of its rule had levelled all opposition, when Death dominates every psychological function and stands above it as its unique and devastating norm—then we recognise madness in its present form, madness as it is posited in the modern experience, as its truth and its alterity.[16]

In this silence which keeps shattering the signifying language of man's soul, the reader needs to recognise his own madness and not question it in others. When June and Babu question it in Sindi, they are oppressed and gradually meet their ends. This is a silence which has its extremity in the gaze of death, and in its terror. Its signifier, then, for the parodoxical purpose of the fictional voice of *The Foreigner* (and of the rest of Joshi's novels) is the acting dispersion of death from the historical event to the life of the characters drifting into the space, its vacancy for that matter. They have no space to polarize with what is on the other side of the edge, to achieve a sense of finitude out of their own physiology, their own economic for their social needs, and their own language to verbalize the divine, however passive, across all of us. The edge, however, endures with the passive, a sense of the distant shimmer, suggested through the bronz Shiva, over Shiela's passive presence in Khemka's utilitarian world. But it is sustained primarily for the entropy of madness in the historical condition, as if its whole activity feeds on the perceptual form of the divine, however distant and passive it may appear to be.

Notes

1. Before the later half of the eighteenth century, language was an organisation of representations of Platonic, ethical (Aristotelian), neo-Platonic and classical frameworks. It was an object of knowledge for man since he existed for the ideal forms of these frameworks. It was indeed, the first sketch of the order of things. In the nineteenth century, language emerged from the experience of man's physiology across his economics and the rationale of social sciences. For a complete reference in this context, see Michel Foucault's *The Order of Things* (London: Travislock Publications, 1970), especially the chapter entitled "Life, labour and language".

2 &

2a Michel Foucault, *The Order of Things*, p. 318.

3. This is a Jamesian reference indicating what he calls the "point of view" technique which he used in *The Portrait of a Lady* rather consciously. In this novel, he succeeds in presenting Isabel Archer's character towards an image of her experienced world of European ethnology. The secondary characters emerge and converge to the possibilities of her own world of things. In many ways, she is the author's authentic image of the modernity of European experience. Joshi's Sindi moves on the same kind of itinerary, although less complex and less signifying.

The Foreigner 189

4. Meenakshi Mukerjee, *The Twice Born Fiction: Themes and Techniques of Indian Novel in English* (New Delhi: Heinemann, 1971) p. 209.
5. O.P. Bhatnagar, "The Art and Vision of Arun Joshi" in *Arun Joshi: A Study of His Fiction* ed. N. Radhakrishnan (Madurai, A Scholar Critic Publication, 1984). In this article he comments, "The novel holds bitter commentary on the much paraded mode of anxiety, rootlessness and isolation as style of life and condemns detachment, renunciation and inaction as panacea for the problems of existance". In this anthology, see also R.S. Pathak's essay entitled "Arun Joshi's Novels: An Indeterminate Search for Meaning in Life." He quotes Edmund Fuller and Spenglerian isolation and meaninglessness in life, perhaps, for the convenience of his ethical terms in modern existence: "He tries to seek, finally, in detachment a solution to his problems." I wonder if Sindi looks to any solutions at all. The novel cannot be easily brushed aside as another work illustrating the much paraded generalization of alienation.
6. For a detailed commentary on the critics of Arun Joshi of 1983 and before, see my essay "The Fiction of Arun Joshi: The Language of Splintered Mirror" in *Ariel* Vol 14/Number 4. 1983. pp. 20–33.
7. This twin birth of man and language refers to a sense of adjacency of man and his creations, humanities and social sciences in Foucault's context of the

archaeology of the historical event. See his *The Archaeology of Knowledge* trans. A.M. Sheridan Smith (London: Travistock Publications, 1972), Part IV.
8. This is Susanne Langer's phrase. She says "The symbolic materials given to our senses, the *Gestalten* or fundamental perceptual forms which invite us to construe the pandemonium of sheer impressions into a world of things and occasions, belong to the "presentational" order. *Philosophy in a New Key: A Study in the Symbolism of Reason, Rite and Art,* (Harvard Univ. Press. 1971), p. 98.

9. This is Michel Foucault' term, indicating that the historical event opens up to the creative artist in making a point of rupture—a discontinuous sign against the past—to give it a form, as it distributes its elements in the mind of the author. The form emerges as the image of exteriority, since every thing interior takes place in shaping the exterior or perceptual surface, anyway. This event goes back in history as an archaeological form, a monumental image of the historical event, a positivity on its own as *difference* from all other forms. See Michel Foucault, *The Archaeology of Knowledge,* Part III.

10. Arun Joshi, *The Foreigner,* (New Delhi, Asia Publishing House, 1968) pp. 3,5. All other references to this novel are indicated by pages numbers in parenthesis in the body of the text.

11. Michel Foucault's idea of the order of things in which man can achieve his "Finitude" with "Life, Labour and Language."
12. Michel Foucault, *The Order of Things*, p. 318.
13. T.S. Eliot's idea of still moment in which what is temporal is arrested in what is timeless. Foucault refers to the same issue in his *Archaeology*.
14. It refers to transformations of what is absent into what is present ; an ordering of the historical event with an artistic rupture with the comtemporary condition of man.
15. R. Rangachari, "T.S. Eliot's shadow on *The Foreigner* in Arun Joshi": *A Study of his Fiction* ed. Radhakrishnan (A Scholar Critic Publication), pp. 1-8.
16. Michel Foucault, "The Human Sciences" in *The Structuralist from Marx to Levi Straus* ed. Richard and Farnanda DeGeorge (Garden City, New York: Doubleday and Company, 1972), p. 272.

RUTH PRAWER JHABVALA: *Heat and Dust*

Brijraj Singh

Had *Heat and Dust*[1] not won the Booker Prize in the year of its publication (1975), or been turned very recently (1983) into a beautiful and successful film by Ismail Merchant and James Ivory, it would still compel critical attention. Reviewers have praised its complex narrative structure which enables Jhabvala to weave scenes from 1923, recreated largely from Olivia's letters to her sister Marcia, with the narrator's diary written in the 1970's. The constant shift of scenes between then and now permits each situation of the past to comment on its counterpart in the present and vice versa; equally important, the characterization of people involved in past situations becomes a subtle and indirect way of illuminating the protagonists of today. Very early in the novel the narrator states modestly if somewhat disingenuously, "This is not my story. It is Olivia's..." (p. 2). But in telling Olivia's story she tells her own; indeed, we cannot hope to understand her except through Olivia, for in *Heat and Dust* the past explains the present. Yasmine Gooneratne has not only studied this aspect of the novel but has also suggested perceptively that Jhabvala learnt the techniques of juxtaposition, splicing and cutting, flashback and fadeout from her experience of writing film scripts for the Merchant-Ivory team, and from the opportunities this experience provided of becoming familiar with the work of film editors.[2]

The oscillation from the past to the present and back again serves to highlight a major concern of the novel—the relationship between then and now, how independent India is different from imperial India in important ways, and how, underlying these differences, is an essential continuity. "Everything is different now," the narrator says at the outset (p. 2), and later quotes a remark of one of Karim's guests to her in London: "Those days had their own charm." (p.98). The novel suggests three perspectives through which the passage of time is to be viewed as it affects India: time decays, time fructifies, and time changes nothing.

Signs of decay are everywhere. The palace at Khatm, the scene of splendour and intrigue and lavish parties and throbbing life, is now shut up, and not even ghosts haunt it. The small State itself is *Khatm*—finished. The Collector's house is now a grimy government office, with its rooms partitioned and walls stained. The Italian marble angel on the grave of the Saunders' baby is mutilated, and the graves themselves, so well tended in 1923, have become unkempt. Even the quality of stationery has deteriorated. Fifty years after they were written, Olivia's letters still retain a scent, but those that the narrator receives from Chid are written on impersonal post office forms and covered with stains and smells. The physical aspect of decay is perhaps more vividly brought out in the film than in the novel owing to the cinema's greater visual appeal; thus the beautiful terrace by the lake where Olivia and the Nawab played musical chairs in the moonlight has become a drab platform of flagged stones by the time the narrator visits it, and Inder Lal's bicycle and tiffin box on the handlebar contrast incongruously with the Nawab's Rolls Royce and Alpha Romeo.

But if the film succeeds in capturing the physical contrasts between then and now more vividly than the book can, the book is able to make other kinds of differences clear in ways that the film misses. The most significant difference is at the level of character. In place of the Nawab as lover we now have Inder Lal. The Nawab was charming and vital and wicked, florid, expansive and commanding, spoiled but generous. Inder Lal, a petty bourgeois the likes of whom did not exist in 1923, is a lowly clerk living in cramped quarters, polite and considerate and yearning for a fuller life, but weighed down by the cares of living, and capable of thinking at the deepest level of his being of little else but the intrigue that surrounds him at his office (p. 126).

The important way in which Jhabvala suggests the difference between the two men and the worlds they inhabit is through a series of contrasts between their Westernization or the lack of it. The Nawab, though politically dependent on the British, can deal with them on terms of some equality. He has style, has travelled abroad, and has English friends. To him it is nothing to order a piano

Heat and Dust

tuner from Bombay, or to serve roasted chickens, quails and potted shrimps at the picnic he organizes for Olivia. Of course his Westernization is superficial. Though perfectly at home in the English language, he speaks an unmistakeably Indian variety with his "I will tell you"'s and "Come here please"'s and "We are not talking with you but with each other." (p.44). When Olivia's husband Douglas hears of her pregnancy, he says, "You'll really do this for me? How brave you are." (p. 155). Contrast this with the Nawab's words on hearing the same news: "Really you will do this for me? . . . You are not afraid? Oh how brave you are!" (p. 152). The words are basically the same, but the Nawab is given to more of them, is more expansive, and more exclamatory.

The self-assured confidence with which he uses an Indian variety of English, not knowing that he has failed to catch the exact accents of the British, is of a piece with the confident manner in which he expresses admiration, first of Olivia's pathetic attempts to play Bach on a miserably-tuned piano at the palace (p. 88), and later of the organ player in a London tea room (p. 177). He does not realize that his acquaintance with Western music is superficial, and would probably not have cared if he had.

However, neither in his failure to speak English like a native, nor in his ignorance of Western music, is the superficiality of his Westernization revealed as completely as in his moral code. Olivia, mistaking him to be a truer gentleman than he really is, can say that he is "almost like one of us" (p. 69), but the other Britishers know better. Saunders is convinced that no Englishman would take revenge on his enemy by first making the enemy's wife pregnant and then encouraging her to elope. While Saunders is a jaundiced observer, there is little doubt that no Englishman in the novel sees his ancestors' greatness as the touchstone and guide of his conduct as completely as does the Nawab. Douglas' family has served India for generations, and Douglas is proud of this fact and conscious of having to uphold family traditions, but never does his sense of family tradition become as consuming a passion with him as the Nawab's obsession with the greatness of Amanullah Khan, and a feeling of inadequacy at being unable to live up to these ideals, do. And just as attitudes to family traditions as the basis of conduct separate the races, so does the fact that in the Nawab's character are to be found ambiguities, depths and surprises which are foreign to the British. Saunders' is a closed mind, Douglas is an honest, upright, and unimaginative man. There are no surprises about them. But the Nawab, outwardly so sophisticated and charming, is not above inciting communal riots and encouraging dacoits to terrorise his own people. There are sides to his life that no Britisher, not even Harry or Olivia, can know or understand.

Superficial though the Nawab's Westernization is, he appears very English—and very impressive—when contrasted with the totally homespun Inder Lal. The narrator is presumably the first foreigner Inder Lal has met; when they go on a picnic together and she unpacks the sandwiches, Inder Lal gets as close as he ever will to sampling Western food; and as for Western art or music, he does not even know that they exist. However, he knows the English language. The novel offers far fewer examples of his speech than it does of the Nawab's—Inder Lal remains an essentially silent and passive character—but from the picnic and seduction scene (pp. 124-28), where he is shown at his most vocal, it appears that his English, while as adequate as the Nawab's was, is just as Indian in its formality, slight verbosity, and the pains it takes to achieve clarity: "Even in a place like this in the middle of the desert, one thousand miles from anywhere, people will come", and again, "How can I say. I am not a magician or other person to read another's thoughts" (p. 126). Inder Lal does not need to be apologetic about his English, but he feels more defensive and insecure about it than the Nawab did. He welcomes the narrator as his paying guest because this will give him a chance to practise his spoken English. He enjoys her company because he knows that his is a small and shrunken world, he yearns to over-come his insularity, and he hopes that the Englishwoman will bring a whiff of the outside world into his life and thus satisfy his yearning for a fuller existence. Indeed, though Jhabvala does not caricature Inder Lal's bounded existence or treat it with irony, she leaves us in no doubt that Inder Lal of independent India has neither the charisma nor the charm of the imperial Nawab. Inder Lal lacks the Nawab's depth and complexity. The Nawab, though politically powerless, wished to dominate persons and events. Inder Lal has no family traditions, no ideals or ambitions. He is incapable of grand gestures, and his moral life amounts to little more than bearing the burdens of a lowly existence with an uncomplaining glumness.

Nothing brings out the contrast between an opulent past and a faded present as well as the two seduction scenes. The Nawab seduces Olivia partly because she is beautiful, partly because, as Major Minnies points out, he is bored, and partly as a revenge upon the British. The seduction is managed with some finesse and passion. The sett-ing is right. Other seductions have taken place in the shrine of Baba Firdaus in the past, because the legend associated with the place leads naturally to thoughts of sex. Olivia is tired by the climb to the shrine, terrified by the dacoits whom she surprises there, feels the commanding power with which the Nawab deals with them, and is herself unable to resist it. The Nawab, always eloquent, overwhelms her with a torrent of words on his favourite subject, the violent and passionate Amanullah Khan. In recounting Amanullah's story the Nawab takes on, as it were, some of his ancestor's attributes; and passion, violence and power culminate in the seduction.

By contrast, the narrator's seduction of Inder Lal is a poor affair. She lays her hand on his, he looks at her "in an entirely different way" (p. 127), and the whole thing is accomplished. Nothing has prepared us for this event: neither the narrator nor Inder Lal has had thoughts that way inclined, and the whole account is devoid of all passion. Indeed, for all that the narrator says that Inder Lal is a very adequate lover, she is aware, too, that fear seems as powerful an emotion with him at the moment of his yielding as lust.

The decline that has occurred between then and now is not confined, in the novel, to Satipur and Khatm. Gooneratne points out that Karim, the Nawab's nephew who lives in London, is so degenerate that he is planning to abet a further Western rape on India. Nor have the English themselves been spared. The Western derelicts who inhabit A.'s hotel in Bombay are a recent phenomenon. Harry hated India, complained against it, and wanted to go back to England, although he was too weak to break free of the Nawab. But, his physical and moral weakness notwithstanding, he was a sympathetic and understanding character. While in India, he had also been very, very happy (p. 172). Not so Chid, a latter-day parody of the Englishman who goes native with a vengeance and ruins his digestion in the process. Both Harry and Chid require medical attention; both, after an initial infatuation with India, experience revulsion. But we are meant not only to see these similarities, but also to feel repulsed by Chid, while Harry has our sympathy. *Heat and Dust* seems to be saying that if the Indians have suffered decline, so have the British. The memorial to the glory that was the Empire is not a continued performance of heroic acts, but, ironically, the cemeteries that can be found everywhere in India (p. 174).

But though aristocratic splendour and grand gestures have been replaced by lower middle class griminess and pettiness, the essence of life in India has not changed. What has happened is that, metaphorically speaking, those who inhabited the servants' quarters in the past have come to occupy the positions that were held by the foreigner and the aristocrat, giving a sense of decline. But basic human realities have remained unchanged. Olivia saw Indians around in India—the servants, the peasants, the traders, the dacoits—but they never impinged on her consciousness. She heard drums beating in the servants' quarters, but showed no interest in what was going on there. She knew that a whole wretched world lay beyond the palace walls, "but why look that far?" (p. 103). Now the palace is in decay and the wretched have inherited India. Though their wretchedness affects their style of functioning, in many essential ways things remain the same.

The barren, rocky landscape between Satipur and Khatm, the heat and dust that greeted Olivia fifty years ago, are there still. Olivia found, when visiting the ladies at Khatm with Beth Crawford, that relations between the races were governed by a strict set of rules: the visitors had to sit in chairs not because they were more comfortable but because it was expected of the Europeans, the visit had to last a certain time, and only certain topics could be brought up in the conversation. The narrator, visiting her landlady fifty years later, enjoys the experience whereas Olivia had been intimidated and bored by it; but rules govern visits still. Like Olivia, the narrator has to sit in a chair when she would have preferred the floor; like Olivia, again, she has to address her remarks to the older lady though she would have liked to include Ritu in her conversation as well. The Saunders' house smelt of death when Olivia visited it, and smells so still, though it is now a rest house. Abortions can still be had on the sly, and methods remain much the same. The abortionists started off by massaging Olivia's stomach, and Maji does the same with the narrator. For the abortionists of today are the descendants of those of yesteryear, and learnt their skills from them.

More significant are the similarities that underlie the differences between the Nawab and Inder Lal. Both have contracted unhappy marriages, the wives of both are mentally ill, and neither has any real communication with his wife. Both the Nawab and Inder Lal feel that they can open their hearts more freely to their white mistresses than to anyone else; yet both are under the control of their mothers, and, when the crunch comes, it is to their mothers that they turn. Both make the same joke to their mistresses when their affairs begin at the shrine of Baba Firdaus.

If the Nawab lives on, in however attenuated a way, in Olivia, Inder Lal lives on in the narrator. Notwithstanding their differences, both are Englishwomen who, without necessarily falling in love with India or Indians, have affairs with Indians and decide to make India their home.

Olivia, whom the narrator describes as not having been in any way exceptional (pp. 159-60), proves, however, to have been capable of great devotion and determination; and the narrator, who is, if possible, even less exceptional, proves no less capable. The narrator says that India changes people (p. 2), and must have changed Olivia (p. 160); she recognizes that India has certainly changed her (p. 2). Like Olivia she, too, abandons the plains to seek refuge in the mountains. She wonders whether Olivia spent her last days embroidering by her window and waiting for her lover to come (p. 175), almost like the Lady of Shalott, we may add, or whether the view of the mountains symbolized a deeper meaning to her (p. 180). We, in turn, may wonder whether the narrator's desire to sequester herself in the monastery marks a retreat from the world, or whether she is really in quest of a meaning symbolized by the mountains, though she herself is not very clear as to what the meaning is, since the mountains are still hidden in mist.

If time decays, and yet paradoxically changes nothing, more paradoxically still it improves and fructifies. Perhaps this is not so parodoxical at all, for the Empire has gone, and therefore though there are outward signs of decay everywhere, not only has human nature remained the same, but the emergence of a new political order has also made possible an efflorescence of the human spirit.

When Olivia comes to India, she has everything going for her. She is young, beautiful, in love, and turns her house into what Harry rightly calls an oasis. But it does not take her long to start feeling bored. Though the Englishmen in Satipur do exciting things, in their own lives they are dull and predictable; and as for the ladies of Khatm, language as well as racial and social barriers make friendships impossible. It is to inject some interest into her life that she starts going out with the Nawab. Not a snob or a racist, though limited by the circumstances of her time, she can envisage the possibility of a friendship with him, for, like E.M. Forster, she believes in the value of human relationships. Indeed, she is a bit like a Forster character from his Mediterranean phase. Her name carries an aroma of Italy; with her music and her yellow cushions and lampshades and her black and white Japanese prints and her attractive little dinner parties, she represents a cultivated sensibility different from the Saunders' morbid moralism or the Crawfords' sunny practicability. Jhabvala hints that Olivia's character needs some warmth to blossom; and blossom it does in her early months in India, when the Indian climate is not unlike the Italian. But as pressures mount, Olivia loses her ability to cope. It is as though, attuned to the uncomplicated world of the Mosque section of *A Passage to India,* she suddenly found herself out of her depth in the Caves or the Temple section. The politics of Empire render the possibility of personal relationships impossible; she is reduced to a pawn in the struggle between the British and the Nawab, and ultimately takes refuge in the hills, away from the British, away from the Indians, and largely ignored by the Nawab. An attractive and well-meaning person, she ends her days as an enigma. Did she occupy a room with a spiritual view in the mountains? Was she a recluse or a visionary, spiritually free or a prisoner, happy or otherwise? We do not know; but we do know that her attempts at bridge-building proved abortive.

Nothing symbolizes this fact better than her physical abortion. For all its glitter, the past was sterile: it could offer no possibilities, lead to no new birth. It had to die.

Another metaphor drives the point home. Heat and dust is not just a physical fact about India, or, as Gooneratne suggests, a symbol of passion. It is also the myth created by the Empire to rationalize its own failures. The Englishman's inability to bear heat and dust becomes a barometer of his inadequacies vis-a-vis India. Harry suffers much more than Olivia, who seems to bear it well; but as the heat increases, her own crisis also crests. Heat and dust increase her boredom and frustration; it is partly because she is so limp from the heat that the refreshing cool of the grove impresses her strongly, and makes her yield to the Nawab.

The narrator experiences heat and dust, too, and remarks that it makes everyone restless and causes a turmoil in her mind (p. 79). But she is far less troubled by it than Olivia was. The film brings this out well: whereas the storm covered everything in Olivia's house with dust, the narrator, when she experiences a similar storm, merely stuffs paper into the cracks in the door, and goes on as before. Indeed, she has a response to the Indian climate that was unheard of in the days of the Raj: while suffering from the heat, she can see that it brings compensations in the form of sweeter mangoes and melons, *gul mohurs,* and jasmine (p. 124).

The images of efflorescence and fructification, which are associated in the narrator's mind with heat and dust, indicate that now that the Empire is dead, interracial relationships can blossom. Unlike Olivia, the narrator is never bored in Satipur, for she has any number of friends ranging from Inder Lal's mother to Maji. Though her visits to Inder Lal's mother are governed by certain rules, she really enjoys them. Olivia had found language a barrier; the narrator applies herself to learning Hindi and is soon able to converse with Indians. Even when language fails, she is able to enjoy having people around, and the "communion" she experiences with them (p. 52) provides a satisfaction she never knew in the loneliness of London. She becomes, in short, part of the Indian scene, accepted and accepting. In such a situation heat and dust mean no more to her than they do to the average Indian; certainly she does not need to invoke them as alibis to explain away failures in communication.

The new relationship with India is symbolized by the narrator's determination to see her pregnancy through. The present is fruitful, and offers promise for the future. It will not die; it will grow into a new life.

The themes of sterility and fertility, as embodied in Olivia's abortion and the narrator's refusal to have one, are suggestively present throughout the novel. The festival of *Pati ki shadi*, or Husband's Wedding Day, is observed by barren women who pray at Babu Firdaus' shrine on that day for a child. Olivia witnesses a dance of the *hijras*, and though she looks as different from them as possible, events prove that there is a similarity between them as well: like the *hijras*, Olivia remains childless. It is not, therefore, surprising that at a subliminal level she should identify with them, for she actually enjoys the dance (p. 123). The narrator, on the other hand, big-boned and flat-chested, looks like a *hijra*. But she is not sterile; therefore, unlike Olivia, she finds their dance pathetic and sad (p. 10). Indeed, it is only when the two appearances of the *hijras* in the novel are related to the theme of fertility and sterility that they come to be seen as integral to the purposes of the novel, rather than as having been brought in merely for the sake of exotic colouring.

The theme of fertility and sterility modulates into that of liberation versus bondage. There are a number of *suttee* shrines in Satipur, and the last *suttee* took place there in Olivia's time. Olivia finds the idea of devotion to one's husband, which is at the back of the *suttee* practice, rather appealing, and is willing to defend the practice itself, at least in theory (p. 59). Figuratively speaking, her incarceration in the mountains is a bit like committing *suttee:* the motive behind her action is, at least in part, devotion to the Nawab; it is also an action which causes the Britishers in Satipur to regard her as though she were dead. She may be said to have died in the bondage of devotion.

Widows in modern India behave differently. The narrator calls Inder Lal's mother and Maji "merry widows" (p. 55); they seem to have sprung to life and freedom only after the death of their husbands. The modern widows of Satipur are far from being *suttee*-like, and this is what gives them a dynamism in the narrator's eyes. The narrator, too, begins to experience a spiritual exhilaration when she abandons Inder Lal and the plains in favour of the mountains: it is as though to gain freedom she has first to become, in some sense, widowed. In other words, the sterile past is associated with the bondage of *suttee,* whereas the present is associated with the freedom and release that widowhood represents in the novel.

The narrator's pregnancy establishes, then, the possibility of meaningful interracial relationships in the present, and promise for the future. At the same time, the novel warns us not to see these possibilities through too rosy a haze. Shortly after the narrator discovers that she is pregnant, she leaves her friends and lover behind in Satipur and takes to the mountains. Her pregnancy seems to have awakened her to the possibility of a spiritual life, and the book ends with her wishing to go to yet higher reaches in the mountains, both physically and metaphorically, and not return to the plains. That is, her pregnancy leads to a spiritual quest, but this quest can succeed only at the expense of social relationships. So long as she lived in the plains, she had friendships but no spiritual vision. But once she feels a spiritual awakening, once she feels that India has possessed her, impregnated her, and freed her, once she feels that she is in and of India, and has India inside her, she abandons all that India has meant to her so far—her communion with other human being, her personal and social levels of existence. Elsewhere I have argued that in *A Passage to India* an unbridgeable dichotomy is created between social and spiritual fulfilment;[3] and Jhabvala seems to do the same. To the question whether it is possible in the present to have the best of both worlds, her answer would seem to be: "No, not yet; no, not here." For present-day India, though fruitful and fertile, cannot be romanticized to the point where it is made capable of fulfilling all levels of existence.

Jhabvala's threefold vision of time in *Heat and Dust* as that which brings to a new birth, preserves, and destroys—as Brahma, Vishnu and Mahesh, in fact—marks a new departure for her. In her other novels she has dealt only with independent India, and with that part of India's history which she has seen shaping with her own eyes. In *Heat and Dust*, however, she studies both the past and the present as a way of getting to understand the present better, and also because she wants to see what in the past is dead and what still survives.

The importance of time in the novel, and the bringing in of a historical perspective, serve to establish a link between *Heat and Dust* and a certain type of pre-Independence English novel about India. Anglo-Indian novelists often saw India as a vale of soul making for the British. India was the crucible in which Englishmen were tried and tested. Some were found fit, and the novelist's attempt was to show what qualities went into the making of a hero. These qualities were, as often as not, those that the novelist, or his age, thought were essential to the success of the Empire. *Heat and Dust* shows that independent India continues to be, as imperial India was, a test for English character; only, the purpose of Jhabvala in subjecting English-men to the test is different. Like her predecessors she, too, wishes to separate the sheep from the goats, but her criterion of success is the character's ability to transcend heat and dust, the bewildering and off-putting external manifestations of India, and give himself or herself over completely to India. To the Britisher who asks: what should I do to be saved? *Heat and Dust* replies that salvation lies in a total surrender to and total absorption in India. Jhabvala believes that many Britishers are asking this question today, and they even realize that they have to turn to India for salvation: how else can one explain the presence of so many seekers in modern India, Chid, the anonymous tourist couple, the hippies in A.'s hotel, and the narrator herself? But though many come, few are chosen. What equipment of character and spirit is required for salvation in and by India is an important concern of the novel.

Dr. Gopal thinks that no Englishman can pass the Indian test, or should even try. India is for Indians only, and not even for them: "I think perhaps God never meant that human beings should live in such a place" (p. 158); and again, " None of you. ...For Indians only! Keep out!" (p. 159). Though the narrator does not agree, Dr. Gopal's words are certainly applicable to a number of Britishers whom we meet in the novel, people who, it is obvious from the first, are failures, like the tourist couple. The narrator thinks that the missionary woman, who has decided to stay on in India to answer what she thinks is Christ's call, though her whole being revolts against India, is a success (p. 159). But Dr. Gopal's words suggest that she may not have heard God's call aright, and would be better off if she went away. Gopal's words apply also to the Crawfords, though not in quite the way he meant them: the Crawfords realize that independent India is no place for erstwhile rulers, and very sensibly decide to leave. Gopal's words apply also to Harry, an aesthetic and likeable but rather spineless young Englishman who comes to the court of an Indian prince not because he is interested in India but out of a spirit of friendship, and is too weak to break these bonds, though he wishes to go back to England. Jhabvala treats him kindly, though she does not gloss over his weaknesses. He is the only one of the 1923 *dramatis personae* alive still, and it may be (though this is never made explicit) that his longevity is the gift that the novelist has granted him in return for the love and devotion he offered to the Nawab. His devotion, his longevity, the fact that he has a mother in England to whom both he and the Nawab write, as also his frank acknowledgement that he hates the imperialists just as he hated his public school, where he was constantly bullied, all parallel events in Forster's life at the Dewas court; and this parallelism is Jhabvala's way of acknowledging the debt that *Heat and Dust,* as indeed all novels on India written by non-Indians, owe to Forster, and suggesting, too, that personal relationships, however desirable, cannot survive the strains of Empire. But for all that Harry was very, very happy in India (p.172), he knew that he could not survive there. He was not made for India, or India for him.

Gopal's words apply with special force to Chid. When we first meet Chid, he appears to have become not only completely Indian but also to be deeply immersed in Hinduism. But the truth is rather different. Far from being a genuine "born again" sanyasi (pp. 20-21), he is a rather silly, naive, ignorant and ill-educated boy who can't even spell (p. 94). He has not really come to India as a seeker, but merely followed the fashion of running away from the West. His spiritualism is bogus: he needs money from home to survive (p. 23), and cannot do without sex, though the narrator naively thinks that his sexual prowess is in some way related to his spiritual attainments (p. 65). His revolt over, aware now of a fact which he had hitherto hidden from himself—that he can't really stand Indian food and Indian smells (p. 139)—and lying sick in hospital, wanting to know nothing and see nothing (p. 158), Chid represents the dangers of what may happen when the wrong kind of Englishman decides to test himself in the Indian crucible.

But if the examples of Child, of Harry, of the missionary woman and the tourist couple, show the truth of Dr. Gopal's words, what about those who do manage to make a home in India, Maj. Minnies, Olivia, and the narrator herself? The question of the Englishman in India fascinates Minnies, who stays on in Ooty after independence and writes a monograph on the subject. He says that the people who are most susceptible to India are precisely those who are endowed with a fineness of character. In other words, people of gross sensibilities cannot love India. In so far as this view rules out from the list of saved people the tourist couple, the missinary, Dr. and Mrs. Saunders, and Chid, he and Dr. Gopal are in agreement, though for different reasons. Both transmit to the gross, the vulgar, or the intolerant India's message: Keep out! But Minnies then goes on to add that the best part of a good man's character, the quality which enables him to respond to India in the first place, is also the weak spot that India discovers and exploits. For Saunders, the weak spot in the English character, which made the Englishman yield to India, was also what made him rotten. For Minnies, the presence of the weak spot is what makes the European a fine human being; but because the finer the human being, the weaker the spot, and the more vulnerable he is to India, the good man must fight against his goodness if India is not to claim him. For if India does, the man will be lost and his goodness destroyed. Minnies, in fact, presents the paradox of the good man who, because he is good, loves India, but for whom India also remains an enemy which has to be constantly fought in order that his goodness may remain inviolate. The way to resist evil becomes, for him, a suppression of all that is best within the self.

Minnies' is a strange stance, as the narrator recognizes (p. 171). Though he claims that he himself has loved India too much, "gone too far over" (p. 170), opened himself too completely to its poetry and its beauty (pp. 148-49), the fact that he always sees India as an antagonist gives the lie to his claims. He has, in fact, gone but one short step towards loving India—which, in terms of the novel, means that he has gone but one short step towards salvation—and then, having stopped there, spent the rest of his life in congratulating himself both on having gone too far in his love affair, and on having been saved in the nick of time. However, the truth is that what he considers to be his salvation is really a sign that, in the vale of soul making that is India, he has been found wanting. He is self-deluded; if he has found a paradise, it is a fools' paradise.

Olivia surrenders herself to India more completely than Minnies could, which is the reason why Dr. Saunders declares that she is rotten, Minnies admires her, and the narrator feels that she is heroic. But Olivia's is a sterile, fruitless surrender; as has already been pointed out, her life in the hills has a question mark hanging over it. Not that she lacks fineness of soul, but the fact of the Empire is not propitious to her surrender. Besides, certain features of her surrender render it less than perfect.

What, then, according to the novel is the perfect surrender to India, and who is capable of it? The answers are to be found in the narrator's life and personality. It is amazing how, once she has got over the fact that the reality of Bombay is different from the Bombay that existed in her imagination (p. 2), she suffers no culture shock at all in India, but takes as naturally and inevitably to Indian life as a fish to water. Her greatest difficulty in Satipur seems to be finding women's sandals large enough for her feet! (p. 9). So quickly and easily does she slip into Indian life, living in a lower middle class home, squatting on the floor, eating Indian food, wearing Indian clothes, adapting her daily routine to the rhythms of India, having Indian friends sleeping with the members of the Inder Lal family out in the open, going to bed in a Sari, and singing hymns, that after just over two months' stay in Satipur she can say that she has merged into the landscape, is part of the town, part of people's lives there, and has been completely accepted (p. 78). No European could have done this, or even tried to, in 1923; no other European character in the novel manages as much today except, perhaps, Chid; but Chid's success in India is apparent rather than real.

Heat and Dust seems to say, then, that in order that the European may succeed in the vale of soul making that is India, he or she must possess certain attributes to start with. He must never reject, he must never assert, he must give and give in, he must accept, and he must not question. Unlike Chid, the narrator never tries to go native with a vengeance, or be other than what she is. Whatever she does comes naturally to her. Though she questions Inder Lal and others on many subjects, she never questions her Indian experiences. When Ritu throws a fit and starts screaming, the narrator helps Inder Lal's mother to control her and take her indoors without any sense of repulsion, horror, or surprise. She sees the mother practising ritual magic on Ritu, and though she does not understand what is going on, does not question it either. She simply takes it for granted. It is this kind of passive acceptance of, and acquiescence to, India that wins her the friendship of Inder Lal's mother and, later, of Maji.

Here lies a problem, with the narrator as well as with the novel. Gooneratne has high regard for the narrator, whom she sees as honest, observant, trustworthy, and morally fastidious, though like her grandfather Douglas she is given to understatement and to not revealing her feeling[4] This view implies that there is a depth to the narrator's character. But the passive acceptance which I have described as characterizing her responses to India suggests just the opposite. If she yields to India without a struggle, is it not because there is nothing in her that she has first to subdue or lay aside? Is not her passive acceptance nothing but a general characterlessness? Though she often goes to the Satipur post office, she seems to have no correspondence or connection with anyone in the outside world. Though she keeps a diary, she confides little that is deeply personal. She allows Chid to make love to her, not because she desires or enjoys it, but just because things work out that way. Her tone, her style, her responses, are flat, neutral, colourless. Take, for instance, the first few sentences with which the novel opens:

> Shortly after Olivia went away with the Nawab, Beth Crawford returned from Simla. This was in September, 1923. Beth had to go down to Bombay to meet the boat on which her sister Tessie was arriving. Tessie was coming out to spend the cold season with the Crawfords. They had arranged all sorts of visits and expeditions for her, but she stayed mostly in Satipur because of Douglas. They went riding together and played croquet and tennis and she did her best to be good company for him. Not that he had much free time, for he kept himself as busy as ever in the district. (p. 1).

The passage is factual and observant, but the writing is pedestrian, and there is no suggestion in it that the writer is capable of imaginative effects, of metaphor, of humour, or of kindness. It is the writing of a person without personality.

The feeling that the narrator is characterless grows when we look into her past life. We know that she lived in London in a flat and felt lonely, but what did she do there? Did she have friends? Or ideas? Or problems? We are not told. Of course it may be claimed that a knowledge of such details is not germane to our reading of the novel, and that besides, the narrator's refusal to divulge any of this information is part of her shy, retiring character. But unless she is given a past, her surrender to India cannot carry much conviction: you cannot become a new person unless you had an old self in you that you have sloughed off. For all her presence in the novel, the narrator remains rather spectral. When Inder Lal asks her why she has come to India, she tells him that she is tired of Western materialism, and, though not specially attracted to Indian spiritualism, hopes to find a simpler and more natural life here (p. 95). Her words seem trite and conventional, cliches, a soulless rehash or precis of other people's experiences rather than a distillation of her own.

Does Jhabvala wish to suggest that only such a person is fit for salvation through India? Or is it rather that the failure is her own, that she wishes to create a favourable character, such as Gooneratne thinks has been created, but proves unequal to the task? I would say the failure is Jhabvala's, and this view finds corroboration in the novelist's inability to deal convincingly with the spiritual aspects of India, especially with Maji.

Maji is supposed to have spiritual powers to which the narrator refers (pp. 163-65); she also suggests that her desire and courage to go through with her pregnancy were due in part to some kind of spiritual force that Maji was able to transmit to her through touch. For the narrator, Maji's spiritual powers are real enough, though she cannot understand them; and that she is not deluded on this score is borne out by the comfort that Maji's touch is able to bring to the dying Leelavati (p. 115). The trouble is that her account of them carries little conviction with us. What seems to have happened is that Jhabvala has heard that some Indians have spiritual and psychic powers, and believes that this may well be the case, though she has not herself investigated the matter. Sensing the need to create a spiritual character in the novel, she creates Maji, and gives her such attributes as she has heard of at second hand. That is why Maji, for all her rumbustious earthiness and good humour, remains unconvincing. It can, of course, be argued that since she is perceived only through the narrator's consciousness, Maji's lack of credibility is to be explained in terms of the narrator's failure to understand her completely. But behind the narrator's failure is the failure of the novelist herself: the narrator fails because Jhabvala has failed her.

Jhabvala's failure, in *Heat and Dust*, with the psychic and spiritual Maji is paralleled by her failure to give the narrator psychological conviction and depth. When the narrator ties a sacred thread at Baba Firdaus' shrine, and later plays a guessing game with Inder Lal, she claims that there is something in her heart that she wishes to disclose to him (p. 127). However, the disclosure is never made . It is possible that she has thoughts that she is prevented from disclosing because Inder Lal loses interest in the game. But more probably, she has no thoughts because Jhabvala is not able to give her any. However Jhabvala does not wish to acknowledge or reveal this fact, and so she gets round the problem by claiming that the thoughts were there, but were never disclosed. The narrator is then made to develop a sudden and wholly unexpected sexual

Heat and Dust

passion for Inder Lal, and through a deliberate and careful fudging of words ("I really had the desire . . . to disclose the contents of my heart. . . . I did have a desire . . . to get close to him") (p. 127), the impression is created that what the narrator originally wanted to disclose was this sexual passion.

The charge against Jhabvala in *Heat and Dust* has to be, then, that she is not able to create a protagonist with a subtle or complex psyche. If critics like Gooneratne think that the opposite is the case, that the narrator possesses the qualities that I find lacking in her, it is because Jhabvala, by using the technique of filtering everything through the narrator's consciousness, is able to foist on the narrator inadequacies which are her own, and then, by suggesting that the narrator is shy and reserved, conceal these inadequacies behind a veil of becoming modesty. She wishes to suggest that the narrator's success in India is because of her quality of wise passiveness; unfortunately, the impression we sometimes get is that this wise passiveness is also a state of vacuity.

Wise passiveness and unquestioning acceptance may be the beginning of the process of salvation through India, but the seeker must undergo further stages. Olivia too, had accepted the Nawab unquestioningly. Where the narrator goes beyond Olivia in her quest is in the dimension of service. She must serve the poorest, make herself more lowly than the lowliest, and annihilate all pride, before she can be vouchsafed a vision. To achieve the heaven that is India, she must first encounter the hell that is India.

The narrator sees Leelavati, a poor beggarwoman, dying in the street. Though the narrator's mental habits have become Indian, and her first response is that Leelavati is not her problem, she is sensitive enough to show concern for her. She tries to raise help, seeks the hospital's assistance, and then turns in desperation to Maji. Between the two of them they are able to comfort Leelavati in her last moments, and help her to die with decency and in peace. The passage describing the death is perhaps the most lyrical in the novel: "As the glow faded and the sky and air and water turned pale silver and the birds fell asleep in the dark trees and now only soundless bats flitted black across the silver sky: at that lovely hour she died" (p. 115).

The second stage in the narrator's growth of charity and service occurs when she cleans the bedpan of the patient in the bed next to Chid's. In helping Leelavati she had been afraid of pollution, but now her fears are gone. Though her act of serving the patient makes everyone, including the patient, regard her as polluted, she has no such feelings. It is through pollution with the poorest of Indians that she gains the possibility of spiritual freedom. This was an experience that Olivia never had, and that is why I said earlier that her surrender to India was less than perfect, and a question mark hung over her days in the mountains. The narrator goes further than Olivia ever did, and is therefore now ready to proceed even higher in the mountains.

Heat and Dust

Gooneratne sees a change for the worse coming over the narrator as a result of her experiences in Satipur. She argues that the narrator loses her detachment and objectivity—as when she takes issue with Dr. Gopal's and Major Minnies' theories—and becomes ultimately self-deluded, a bit mad. Whereas earlier she had recommended psychiatric treatment for Ritu, Maji had recommended a pilgrimage. In starting off on her own pilgrimage at the end, the narrator is revealing her disintegration, her own need for psychiatry.

It is difficult to agree with this interpretation. Hitherto colourless, passive, and lacking in psychological depth, the narrator grows into possession of positive qualities through her acts of love. Leelavati's plight causes her to abandon her usual passivity and exert herself for another person; her taking issue with Minnies is not, therefore, indicative of a loss of objectivity and restraint, but reveals a new-found spirit. It is this spirit that makes her determine to leave Satipur, to have her baby, and, at the end of the book, to keep on climbing. When we last see her, she is on her way to the ashram where the swamis are cheerful and sincere. There she will presumably find laughter, which she has not experienced much so far, and this laughter will bring her one step nearer divine laughter.

Heat and Dust is, of all post-independence novels on India written by non-Indians, the most significant analysis, after *The Siege of Krishnapur* (though a good way behind), of the qualities required by the foreigner who wishes to be saved through India, and the most unequivocal assertion of the power of India to save. Having lived long enough in India to recognize this power, and to recognize, too, that she was the wrong kind of foreigner for India, Jhabvala embodied in the narrator what she thought were the right kind of qualities, thus making the narrator everything that she herself is not. The homage to India as saviour having been paid, she chose a different path for herself, and started a new life in New York.

Notes

1. Ruth Prawer Jhabvala, *Heat and Dust* (London: John Murray, 1975). All citations are from this text.
2. Yasmine Gooneratne, *Silence, Exile and Cunning: The Fiction of Ruth Prawer Jhabvala* (Hyderabad: Orient Longman, 1983), p. 218, pp. 261-99, *passim*.
3. Brijraj Singh, "Mrs. Moore, Prof. Godbole and the Supernatural: Some Comments on *A Passage to India*," *The Literary Criterion* XV. 2 (1980), pp. 44-53.
4. For Gooneratne's discussion of the narrator, see *Silence, Exile and Cunning*, pp. 222-30.

CHAMAN NAHAL: *Azadi*

Lakhmir Singh

I

The partition of India in 1947 was such a cataclysmic event for the country that people who had suffered then or were even witness to the horror and violence of those fateful days still shudder to recall those happenings. No other event in the history of this country had created so tremendous an impact on India's intellectuals and writers who continue to be haunted by it even today, after more than three decades. Even a writer like R.K. Narayan who has always scrupulously steered clear of political themes, brings in the Partition, albeit partially, in one of his novels *Waiting For the Mahatma.*

Punjabi writers in English, Hindi, Punjabi and Urdu come to this theme again and again, perhaps because Punjab suffered the most on account of the partition. Nanak Singh, Kartar Singh Duggal, Amrita Pritam and several others have written novels, short stories and poems dealing with the trauma of the division of the country. Amrita Pritam's *Pinjar* (translated in English as 'The Skeleton' by

Khushwant Singh) and her poem 'Aj Aakhan Waris Shah Noo' (I invoke Waris Shah Today) have moved the people on both sides of the border so deeply that even today when they read the poem they weep for what they themselves had done to each other—a sign of the shame and disgrace which have descended on us from those fateful days. The Hindi novelists Yashpal (*Jhoota Sacha*) and Bhisham Sahni (*Tamas*) have authentically treated the harrowing experiences of the Partition days. And Qurratullain Haider's *Aag Ka Darya* is outstanding among the Urdu novels on this theme. Among the Indian writers in English, Khushwant Singh's *Train to Pakistan* (1956), Attia Hussain's *Sunlight On a Broken Column* (1961), and Manohar Malgonkar's *Distant Drums* (1960), and *A Bend in the Ganges* (1964) are some of the better novels about the Partition.

An evidence of the continuing and undiminished interest in this theme is to be found in Salman Rushdie's *Midnight's Children* (1981) and Sharaf Mukkadam's extensive treatment of it in *When Freedom Came* (1982).

Truly speaking, so far the theme of the Partition has not been exploited in all its ramifications, not at least by Indian writers in English. It is a theme with epical dimensions and deserves to be treated at the level of *War and Peace*. A great novel about the Partition will be an epic in prose. Chaman Nahal's *Azadi* is important in this context that it is by far the most extensive and perhaps the most authentic novel about the Partition in English.

Nahal, a professor of English at the University of Delhi has written four novels. He has a penchant for historical events and his last novel *The Crown and the Loin Cloth* (1981) is about Gandhi's non-violent struggle against the British Empire. *Azadi,* written in 1975 nearly twenty-eight years after the Partition is still his best known novel.

II

Azadi, meaning 'freedom', takes into account the various events leading to the Partition, the actual event itself and its aftermath. The story is related to certain historical events of great importance and their impact on ordinary people—thus creating two narrative levels, the historical and the human, both merging at crucial points to make the narrative effective.

There is nothing unusually complex in the plot and structure of *Azadi*; it is linear and chronological. The story opens on June 3, 1947 with an announcement by the then Viceroy, Lord Mountbatten's declaring the division of the country into two parts—India and Pakistan; it ends with the assassination of Mahatma Gandhi on January 30, 1948. *Azadi,* thus deals with eight tumultuous months in the history of the Indian subcontinent. The impact of some other historical events preceeding this period is also discernible. Interspersed in the novel are references to the Jalianwala Bagh tragedy, Quit India Movement, the Cripps Mission, the Radcliffe Boundary

Commission, the Interim Government with Nehru as Prime Minister and the Sikh demand that the river Chenab should be the boundary between India and Pakistan. There are frequent references to Gandhi's offer to Jinnah for a home-land for Muslims within an independent India itself. *Azadi* clearly deals with a momentous period of our history.

Azadi, however, does not merely give us a historical document. The great actors involved in the drama of this time—Mountbatten, Rajaji, Jinnah, Gandhiji, Nehru and a host of other national leaders are all present but none of them appears in person in the novel. They are all described through the reactions of the people.

Nahal's purpose is not to depict history but to describe the impact of the historical tragedy of the Partition on ordinary people. *Azadi* is, in fact, the story of millions of people uprooted from their homes for no fault of their own and this story is symbolised in the person of Lala Kanshi Ram and his family and the pain that they go through during the process of this upheaval in their lives and their alienation from their own home-land. Lala Kanshi Ram is a wholesale dealer in grain, whose interest in politics is skin-deep and whose only deviation from routine business is to attend the meetings of the local Arya Samaj. He has lived in Sialkot, a small town, for years, has prospered there and is unwilling to leave even after the Partition is announced. An Arya Samajist to the core, at one stage the thought of converting himself to Islam crosses his mind, so great is the compulsion to stay

Azadi

on in his native town. He is mild-mannered and has always pulled on well with his Muslim friends; in fact his dearest friend is a Muslim, Chaudhari Barkat Ali. Never does it occur to him that he can ever be unwanted in his own native place. Lala Kanshi Ram finally leaves his birthplace like other Hindus and Sikhs. His daughter becomes a victim of communal riots; there is in fact no family left unscattered, no family that does not lose a near and dear one. Like millions of other Punjabis, he travel on foot to India with his wife Prabha and son Arun, moves from city to city—Amritsar, Ambala—and finally arrives in Delhi to suffer more humiliation. His story represents the story of a whole nation, of millions who were forced to leave their homes and to whom *azadi* brings only untold misery and an uncertain future.

The plot of *Azadi*, although conventional in nature, is, structurally speaking, symmetrical and well organized. The novel is divided in three parts entitled as The Lull, The Storm and The Aftermath—all suggestive and symbolic of the three distinct stages in the narrative. 'The Lull' describes the peace and communal harmony among the people of Sialkot before the idea of partition captures the imagination of some Muslim zealots. It also registers the reactions of common people to the imminent partition, and describes the simmering tensions underlying the calm.

In fact, the first three chapters effectively describe the slow building up of tension and the psychological responses of a variety of individuals involved in the situation.

They all wait, with almost suspended breath, for the all-important announcement of Mountbatten for a division of the country. Kanshi Ram who normally does not talk to any one while going through the daily ritual of 'reading' his newspaper excitedly asks his wife's views although she has none. Shopkeepers—Hindus and Muslims—all close their shops early, to be on time in their homes to listen to the broadcast. Prabha Rani and Isher Kaur cook early. Kanshi Ram, Prabha Rani, Isher Kaur, Arun and Niranjan Singh, all gather in their landlady Amarvati's room who alone owns a radio. Although they know what it is going to be, they still hope that the demand for Pakistan will not be conceded. And when the announcement (in English) finally comes, nobody except Lala Kanshi Ram's college going son Arun understands a word of it. So stunned is Arun himself that he lifts his two fingers instinctively and mutters the word 'Partition'. Everybody in the room mutters the word 'Partition', keeps his thoughts to himself, and clings to the one nearest as if seeking some kind of protection. A sense of betrayal grips one and all. They do not listen to Nehru, Jinnah, and Baldev Singh who speak after the Viceroy. Nehru sounds so unconvincing, so incredible. A thousand thoughts cross Lala Kanshi Ram's mind. What have the leaders done? Have they not thought of the security of millions?

The same announcement is greeted with glee and rejoicing by the Muslims who celebrate the occasion with fireworks. Their jubilation is in sharp contrast to the eerie silence that prevails in the Hindu localities. Abdul

Azadi

Ghani, the Muslim hookah manufacturer abuses the Hindu shopkeepers in the choicest Punjabi words. The Muslims get so wild at the announcement that they take out a procession—not yet to kill Hindus but to humiliate them. The processionists pass through various Hindus localities, processionists pass through various Hindus localities, dancing the bhangra, shouting slogans. Hindus and Sikhs only sit helplessly in their homes.

'The Storm' describes the excruciating experiences of the uprooted people in refugee camps and on their way to India. This part unfolds the drama of violence of all sorts, of the atrocities committed on these innocent people, arson, murder, abduction, rape. Also described is the none-too-pleasant experience of these people in their own free country and the indignities they face at the hands of an indifferent and callous bureaucracy. 'The Aftermath' attempts to delineate the inevitable reconciliation of these people to their lot. The prosperous merchant of Sialkot is happy to get a single room with a roof of corrugated sheets where at least he can sleep. Even this little favour is denied to hundreds of others. By and large, the refugees are treated as outsiders; some people may be sympathetic but feel all the same that these quarrelsome Punjabis should look for their livelihood in some small town in Punjab and not in the capital city of Delhi.

Azadi, in a technical sense, is a well-integrated novel, with a story full of human interest, a well-structured plot that is carefully developed in spite of its ready-made historical material.

III

In a novel of this nature fidelity to experience is a positive virtue and *Azadi* reproduces the lacerating experiences of the affected people in an authentic manner. *Azadi* is realistic; no sentimental nostalgia is betrayed and no attempt at idealisation is made. Nahal shows the worst side of the Partition, the brutalisation of a mass of people through mass violence, mass rapes, arson, loot, plunder, murder and relates with documentary sharpness the agonising experience of the people on way to India.

The novel, in fact, draws its main strength from powerfully realistic, precise and intimate narrations of the communal carnage of 1947. It paints a powerful picture of the character and anatomy of the disturbances which usually began on a low key, with rumours and unfounded stories spread by interested persons. And with the rumours began isolated incidents of violence which became forerunners of the storm to follow. In the beginning a small cosy town like Sialkot remained free from such incidents though bigger towns like Lahore, Multan, Amritsar and Jalandhar were already burning. In this town, Hindus, Sikhs and Muslims have lived together in harmony for generations. But with the announcement of Pakistan begin the stray incidents and the result is that lonely Hindus and Sikhs are waylaid and killed:

> In no case was the victim allowed to survive the attack and tell what happened; he was stabbed to death. The

killing was invariably done with a knife and often the knife, the large blade driven clear through, was left in the body of the victim. Where the victim survived the first blow, he was repeatedly stabbed in the chest and the abdomen (*Azadi*, Arnold-Heinemann... p. 126).

Such stray incidents staged with a clinical efficiency come handy to the politicians and the vested interests and that leads to communal riots. The whole town of Sialkot ultimately is engulfed by communal conflagration. The Muslim refugees who have come from East Punjab, have their own tragic tales to tell with the result that even in Sialkot, in spite of age-old cordiality between all communities, a killing spree begins. The leaders only accelerate the forces of destruction. Chaudhari Barkat Ali, a Muslim friend of Lala Kanshi Ram and a secular person, minces no words when he prompts Kanshi Ram to leave his home in Sialkot and tells him categorically:

> ... every day hundreds of refugees from India continue to arrive with tales of terror and disgust. Whatever is happening here in Sialkot, things very much like that are happening on the other side too... let's make no mistake about it ... When refugees with stories of personal misfortunes land here, the politicians use them to their advantage to fan up further hatred. (140).

In the town of Sialkot, even when Hindus and Sikhs are escorted to refugee camps, they are attacked and looted. Lala Kanshi Ram's shop is plundered and what shocks him most is that one of the culprits is none other than Abdul Ghani whom he has helped on a number of occasions. Life in the camps is simply unbearable. Hindus and Sikhs wait there for other convoys to come before they can leave for their own country. What comes, however, are trains full of dead bodies. In one of the attacks on trains Kanshi Ram's daughter Madhu and her husband are killed and he cannot even get their bodies. Kanshi Ram sends his son in search of their bodies but Arun is horrified at the death-like silence at the railway yard. Nahal describes this ghastly scene as seen by one from close quarters

> The dead had been removed from the train and dumped there without sentiment or concern. It so happened many of them had their arms around each other or they were holding each other with their legs. And in the disintegration the fire brought to them, there was a constant movement in the heaps. Arms were climbing up or they were sliding down. Legs were yielding their hold or they were burying themselves deeper. And the eyes of one skull seemed to look into the eyes of another and send unspoken messages. For the other skull would nod, in a way saying it had quite understood. (184)

Azadi

In such circumstance women's honour is the cheapest commodity. They suffer most humiliating insults even as the exchange of population goes on after 15 August, 1947, presumably under protection and security. At night the convoys of the refugees are attacked, men are killed and women taken away. In town after town Hindus and Sikh women are paraded naked in the bazars, with hundreds of men, old and young, doing dances by their sides, passing obscene, vulgar remarks on their private parts. The description of this parade at Jasowal is one of the most realistic scenes in *Azadi:*

> A number of abducted Hindu and Sikh women were in their custody. Many of the kidnapped women disappeared into private homes. A lone Muslim dragged a woman away, and kept her for his exclusive use. Or he took her with the consent of other Muslims, converted her to Islam and got married to her. The rest were subjected to mass rape, at times in public places and in the presence of large gatherings. The rape was followed by other atrocities, chopping off breasts and even death. Many of the pregnant women had their wombs torn open. The survivors were retained for repeated rapes and humiliations until they were parcelled out to decrepit wrecks—the aged, the left overs who could not find a wife or to those Muslims who wanted an additional wife. In the meantime more women were abducted and the cycle was repeated all over again. (239).

A remarkable feature of *Azadi* lies in the objectivity and impartiality that Nahal maintains in portraying the communal riots. The novel in fact gives a picture of these riots in their totality, without presenting a Hindu or Muslim point of view. Nahal blames both the communities for losing their sense of balance and sanity. Where Hindus are in a majority, they indulge in sadistic animalism, and kill and brutalize Muslims as Muslims do where they are in a majority. Reprisals go on both sides. The worst in both the communities are full of communal frenzy and the best are silent and helpless. On reaching Amritsar Lala Kanshi Ram finds the Hindus doing to Muslims precisely what Muslims had done to them. Here Muslims are subjected to the same humiliation—their women are paraded naked, gang-raped with the police and security forces as mute and silent spectators. A train full of Muslims is derailed at Ambala, the survivors are taken out and done away with. "They were laid out beside the track one dead next to another, and they were covered with sheets. It was clear from certain sheets there was only a child below, the corpse was so small" (334), Lala Kanshi Ram's words to his wife put everything in a proper perspective: "Each of those girls in that procession at Amritsar was someone's Madhu ... We are all equally guilty" (339).

Underlying all the harrowing experiences that Nahal describes, a healthy optimism and a sort of moral vision permeate *Azadi*. When communal frenzy, by and large, takes the better of Hindus, Sikhs and Muslims, a small residue of basic human values still remains. Humanity redeems itself through Chaudhari Barkat Ali, a close friend

Azadi

of Lala Kanshi Ram, who helps him at every step. In this gravest hour, Kanshi Ram turns to Barkat Ali only. Barkat Ali remains attached to Kanshi Ram and his family when Hindu and Muslims are completely torn asunder. He even pleads, though ineffectively with his Muslim brothers, to do no harm to innocent Hindus. The inhabitants of the village Jassar on Pakistan border do not attack the foot convoys of the refugees and are surprisingly sympathetic. They "only stood and stared. Even anti-Hindu or anti-Sikh slogans were not shouted by them. Instead of attacking the convoy, some of the inhabitants of Jassar went inside their homes and brought water for the thirsty. Some waved and said, 'Khuda hafiz'. Most only looked on" (320).

IV

Azadi depicts a tragedy of great magnitude of thousands of people who are victims of forces that are formidable and utterly beyond their own control. Those who suffer are mostly blameless, and those who inflict the suffering too are victims since they hardly know why they are doing it. Freedom entails so much suffering in its wake that it is looked upon as a curse for sometime at least. *Azadi* scores in terms of realistic portraiture but more vividly than this, it is the portrayal of mixed multifarious response of people in the grip of situations created by powerful forces. Lala Kanshi Ram, his family and others, Amarvati, Niranjan Singh, Chandni, Sunanda are all good average people who are interested in their routine daily life, with no concern as to who rules the country. Their interest in freedom is peripheral—they venerate their heroes like Bhagat Singh but they also look at the English with awe and wonder.

Lala Kanshi Ram has always been a good Arya Samajist, dutifully entering his mother language as Hindi in the relevant census columns, though he speaks robust Punjabi, and writes in Urdu. He wants India to regain its pristine glory all right but also likes to be seen in public with the English officers. He has been to jail once for a day only though in connection with a sale-tax strike. He is found of talking about that day and loves to have the 'aura of a recolutionary around him'. When the announcement of partition is made, he can only find fault with the cunning monkey race who have brought them to this disastrous state. He is unwilling to leave his home, even after his wife and son have packed every thing to go to the refugee camps. He feels broken. "The pinch was he should have to give up this land, this air. That's where the hurt lay. He breathed deep, filling his lungs with the air of the town to their utmost capacity and tears welled up in his eyes. How could he give this earth up" (132). The amicable Lala Kanshi Ram is harsh to even Davidson, a good Englishman, who is a friend of Arun and who helps them in many ways at the refugee camp. "I am an old man and I cannot begin all over again," sums up not only Lala Kanshi Ram's but a whole nation's tragedy and predicament.

To Arun, the creation of Pakistan brings an end to his romance with Nur, daughter of Chaudhari Barkat Ali. Their relationship cannot survive the crisis of the Hindu-Muslim divide. Arun knows that he has to leave Sialkot, and though Nur suggests him to embrace Islam, he cannot break all his other ties. More than anybody else, Arun knows the inevitable. Life in camps shakes him further. His response to the new situation is that of a disillusioned person. "He knew the conspiracies of politicians behind the whole move Why else would they rush into azadi at this pace— an azadi which would ruin the land and destroy its unity? For the creation of Pakistan solved *nothing.*" (96). His later romance with the low-caste Chandni in the refugee camp is meant to signal his greater maturity which Nahal tries to show, rather unconvincingly, since Arun's love affairs have a sort of discordant role in the context of the national tragedy being depicted, in the following comment: "He had found a new identity for himself, an identity which had partly been thrust on him, an identity which partly he had worked out for himself metaphysically." (233).

The tragedy in the life of young Niranjan Singh is of a different nature. He dislikes cowardice but in his helplessness suffers silently like a caged tiger. Since Sikhs have a distinct identity and are easily recognisable, Niranjan Singh is advised by one and all to shear his long hair in the interests of his family—his beautiful wife is expecting her first child. Being a devout Sikh, this idea is altogether abhorrent to him but on repeated persuasions, he agrees to do so. But on the day he is to cut his hair short, he quietly slips from his tent, gathers dry wood and burns himself to death, with the words ... "Life I'll gladly lose, my Sikh dharma I won't". In such rare moments in the novel, man's personal tragedy transcends the larger tragedy of the community and leaves a deeper impression on the reader's mind.

The *Aftermath* in *Azadi* further accentuates this human tragedy. Lala Kanshi and others who kissed the earth of their beloved free India, find themselves only as aliens and outsiders, who are unwanted here. So intense is their feeling of alienation that they lose their power of communication. The proud whole-sale-merchant of Sialkot even weeps before a custodian officer to get himself allotted a single room. He finds the officers as cruel as the murderers back home. Kanshi Ram, Prabha Rani, Arun, Amarvati, Sunanda, all keep their thoughts to themselves, so powerful is the feeling of loneliness in them. But meanwhile life goes on its relentless course caring little for little people.

V

As stated earlier, Nahal looks at the whole situation as a tragedy of great magnitude, where millions of innocent people become victims of formidable forces. Even the theme of independence becomes secondary in the face

Azadi

of this tragedy. But the biggest victim of the Partition was the composite Punjab culture. *Azadi* portrays the gradual disintegration of the collective Punjabi consciousness—the feeling of belonging to one place, the feeling of doing the same dances, that of singing the same songs. How fragile did it all prove! How tenuous did it become under pressure! *Azadi* probes all this.

From the first page onwards *Azadi* emphasises the common bonds among Hindus, Muslims and Sikhs in Sialkot (and naturally the rest of Punjab)— a sense of *Punjabiat* that held them together. This aspect of the novel may be missed by some Western or even Indian readers, but is not less important nonetheless. Though Hindus declared their mother language as Hindi, Muslims Urdu—and he was taught Urdu by his father and the village school teacher and neither was a Muslim. Everybody learnt Urdu. And Lala Kanshi Ram could abuse only in Punjabi: "All right, all right, Hindi is my language, if you say so. But it is a senile drivel compared to Punjabi if you ask me. Even Urdu comes nowhere near the vigour and plasticity of Punjabi. You are too damned concerned with nafasat, with gentility, to be able to say anything effective. But Hindi, my God, Hindi was a joke." (21-22).

There were other bonds too. The year of the Punjabis began with Baisakhi—the day of rejoicing for one and all when the harvest is done. They sang the same folk songs on marriages and other occasions, and danced Bhangra in the same way and with the same vigour and vitality. They participated in each other's festivals without rancour, open-heartedly and with gusto, as only Punjabis could do. The schools and colleges in Punjab were denominational—Islamia college, Arya Samaj College, Khalsa College, but all admitted students regardless of their religion. But gradually chauvinism began to take the better of all. Lala Kanshi Ram and Abdul Ghani—the two neighbouring shopkeepers had never thought on communal lines. But a couple of years before the Partition a schism began to come in their relationship.

> So there was utter harmony among them, and the fact that Ghani was a Muslim and Lala Kanshi Ram a high caste Hindu never entered their heads. They spoke a common tongue, wore identical clothes, and responded to the weather, to the heat and the first rains, in an identical manner. If they worshipped different gods it was in the privacy of their homes, except when Ghani made a spectacle of himself by joining Tazia marches at the time of Muharram once a year and beating his breast in the public. But then, didn't Lala Kanshi Ram make a spectacle of himself too, when he joined the lalas of bazaar in throwing colour on others during Holi? No, thought Lala Kanshi Ram, they were not Muslims or Hindus they were Punjabis (54).

Azadi scores over other 'Partition' novels because Nahal understands the Punjabi ethos and portrays it

Azadi

intimately and profoundly. This is the main strength of *Azadi*. Khushwant Singh too understands it equally well but unfortunately treats it rather superficially in *Train to Pakistan*. Malgonkar and others barely touch it in their novels about the Partition. For Punjabis, more than the loss of life and property, the Partition meant a loss of identity. *Azadi* comes to terms with this crisis of identity.

For depicting the trauma of the Partition, for its superb delineation of the anguish of the people, for revealing the gradual erosion of the Punjabi consciousness, as also for showing the communal frenzy in its worst aspect, *Azadi* should be considered as a Partition novel of some distinction.

ANITA DESAI: *Fire on the Mountain*

Malashri Lal

At a recent symposium hosted by the Commonwealth Institute, London, Anita Desai focussed on issues concerning 'Indian Women Writers'[1]. While considering the several historical and sociological factors responsible for the insufficiencies, both qualitative and quantitative, in women's literature, Desai spoke of the "low rate of literacy", the lack of a "literary tradition" and "an accompanying lack of the critical faculty."[2] Tracing the evolution of women's writings in the context of the Indian family background, Desai maintained that only the present generation of women, indeed a privileged few within it, enjoyed privacy and solitude which were conditions necessary to literary creativity. However, given favourable conditions, women can render their sentiments in fictional form while deriving their material from social and personal experiences: "Literature can't be torn away from the fabric of life as though it were a decoration or an excrescence—it is woven into it, inextricably."[3] Desai's own novels offer reasonably good examples of the limitations as well as the possibilities in the writings of Indian women. To extend Desai's metaphor of 'the fabric of life,' her novels have the texture of raw silk; rich and somewhat uneven, the knots are visible and one may not wish them away.

Anita Desai's literary career began with *Cry The Peacock* (1963) and extends through eight novels to her most recent one, *In Custody* (1984). These contain some remarkable portrayals of women—Nanda Kaul (*Fire on the Mountain*), Sita (*Where Shall We Go This Summer?*), and Bim (*Clear Light of Day*); an authentic rendering of the turbulence of Calcutta in *Voices in the City;* and a deceptively simple story about children, *The Village by the Sea.* Although the range of subjects is wide—urban domestic life, Gandhism, social exploitation, Indian immigrants abroad—Desai's approach is always and invariably through the mind of a sensitive, high-strung woman given to attitudes of melodrama. Briefly speaking, the plots are thin, the characterization is complex. The psychologically complex, occasionally neurotic woman's view of socially 'ordinary' situations creates the dramatic tension in the novels. And since a great deal is assumed to happen within the splendid labyrinth of an eccentric mind, a suitable mode for the novelist's expression of it is metaphor and symbol. Desai's propensity towards image-making and her recourse to such indigenous sources as the monsoon, the cow, the eagle and the cricket, have often been commented upon. R. S. Sharma's opinion, "There is a sustained effort in her writing to evolve a set of symbols, images or myths,"[4] concurs with Madhusudan Prasad's comment, "In her novels, she has generously employed symbols and images, charged with tremendous significance"[5] However, in undertaking such a view of Desai's art, one is necessarily examining particulars within the scope of single novels, then placing the examples together in order to discern a repetitive structural pattern for the composite whole of Desai's fictional creations. Laudable as this effort is, for it places Desai evaluatively in the contemporary literary scene—and necessary though it may seem when a writer has won the National Academy of Letters Award and been nominated for the Booker Prize—it ignores Desai's own interest in women as products of sociological imperatives.[6]

Desai's statement that "Indian women novelists are still exploring their feminine identity and trying to establish it as something worth possessing,"[7] not only emphasizes the present pre-occupation of the writers but also sees this as a continuous review of femininity in its social context. The transference of the writer's pre-occupation from herself to her protagonists is logical and inevitable. With reference to Desai, one then begins to see the novels as conjectures on feminism and not just as variations on the literary exercise of plot, character and symbolism.

This sets the premise for an interpretation of *Fire on the Mountain* (1977) as a fictional rendering of feminist attitudes in India, and here I use the word 'attitude' to denote modes of thought resulting from a complex of social, historical and personal factors operating simultaneously. Hence, Nanda Kaul—the novel's principal figure—an elderly widow who had suffered from "the nimiety, the disorder, the fluctuating and unpredictable excess" (30) of domestic duties, and in old age, begins upon a "reduced and radiantly single life" (31), depicts a theoretical feminism.[8] In her is the desire to escape traditional constraints but she lacks the volition to do so. Nanda's contemporary, Ila Das, has remained single and found a career by the cumulative accident of circumstances, but having accepted employment, she attends to her tasks conscientiously. Her social constraints are minimal but, like Nanda, she lacks assertiveness. Nanda's great-granddaughter, the adolescent Raka, is, by contrast to the elder women, a person guided only by her instincts and distrustful of society. She is a figure of incipient, radical feminism in which repose the possibilities of self-awareness as well as self-destruction. The fact that two women in the novel are considerably older than the third suggests a chronology in feminist attitudes. Indeed, I wish to infer that the novel has conceptual richness. The plot of *Fire on the Mountain* with its trappings of rather obvious bird and animal images, and the novelist's dramatizations of pitiful eccentricities of character, are scattered elements of that conceptual richness which informs the meditations on feminism.

Nanda Kaul dominates the narrative as its central consciousness. Just as she tries to repel all physical intrusions upon her old and 'pared' existence at Carignano and fails in her attempt, so her peace of mind is assailed by diverse, conflicting and painful memories. Though Anita Desai does not reveal Nanda's age, there is a fair indication of it in the reference to the purchase of Carignano soon after 1947. Apparently, this idyllic hillside cottage, 'shaded by pine-branches' and banked by the shadow of 'dense apricot trees' had been the scene of much colonial errantry. In the second chapter of *Fire on the Mountain,* Desai gives an account of the building of Carignano in 1843 by Colonel Macdougall and its subsequent occupancy by a 'long line of maiden ladies.' Then, "It was 1947. Maiden ladies were not thought to be safe here any more" (9). The town 'went native' and Nanda Kaul, probably middle-aged at the time, bought the old house while she continued to live with her husband, the vice-chancellor at 'a small university town in Punjab,' and attended to her multiple duties as housekeeper to her children, grand-children, relatives and visitors. This phase of her life is told retrospectively. As the novel begins, Nanda, now old but "keeping her back as straight as a rod" sighs contentedly on her first day at the cottage; "it was the place, and the time of life, that she had wanted and prepared for all her life"(3).

It is obvious then that Nanda Kaul represents a fairly descernible stance in Indian feminism as documented in social histories and biographies pertaining to the early twentieth century, a feminism which supports the domestic role of women while recognizing their secret longing for an opportunity to function individually in the world outside the home. The mood is not of rebellion but calm acceptance of a sequence in women's lives— daughter, perhaps the beneficiary of an 'English' education, then wife and member of a joint-family and committed to its collective obligations, and finally in old age, wife or widow with the option to strengthen the inherited conventions or to divert individual energy to social work with the acquiescence of the family.[9]

Nanda Kaul's attitude in 1947 or thereabouts, when she buys Carignano and begins to harbour dreams of liberation, is reflected in personal documents of at least two historical counterparts. Sudha Mazumdar, born in 1898, was raised in a conservative Bengali home yet given the benefits of an English schooling so that she may be a worthwhile bride to a civil servant, a good teacher to her children and a model housewife in a joint family.[10] While fulfilling all these roles dutifully, Sudha Mazumdar continued to maintain a notebook in which she recorded the significant episodes of her life and occasionally her response to them. One recording voice is that of the woman who accedes uncritically to the demands of the family and declares that "the happiest phase of a woman's life" is when she is "the honoured mistress of (her husband's) home"[11] The other voice notes that she "does not idealize the old system." One may sense an inner conflict here, and yet, in the historical context, perhaps there was none, only a waiting for the appropriate time when intellectual urges may be nurtured. And at a later date, this thoughtful woman, so calmly aware of what one today calls 'the feminist conflict' between home and selfhood, took an interest in social work and also translated the Ramayana into graceful English.

Of a model somewhat different from Sudha Mazumdar is Hansa Mahta, honoured as a pioneer of women's education in India.[12] Born in 1897, she played an active role in the politics of her time and, whenever possible, spoke up for the special needs of women. Long before the words acquired a slogan-like ring, Hansa Mehta declared: "It is always desirable for a woman to feel herself economically independent."[13] And yet, the economic independence as well as the desirability of education was perceived within the framework of a woman's position as housewife and mother. Consequently, the formalizing of 'Home Science' as an academic discipline emerged from statements such as this: "Very little thought has been given to train women for the most important role they have to play, viz., that of a home-maker."[14] The social determinants are obvious in the corollaries to a plan for educating women: the dangers of "women's intellectual development" had to be counteracted by strengthening cultural and aesthetic traditions, euphemistically called "appreciation of beauty"—no doubt, lessons in music, art, needlework and languages.[15]

The dialectic cited above in the representative opinions of Sudha Mazumdar and Hansa Mehta belongs to what I have called theoretical feminism—the opposition between the demands of a family and an individual is recognized in the context of an Indian woman's adult life but dangerous speculations about choosing one or the other are brushed aside by a comfortable acceptance of the 'inevitable' chronology of life cycles. This is a position of compromise

Fire on the Mountain

between tradition and activism, domesticity and singleness, and this is the position in which Anita Desai places Nanda Kaul.

A retrospective account of Nanda Kaul's life shows her at the centre of a bustling joint-family:

> ... She had presided with such an air as to strike awe to visitors who came to call and leave them slightly gaping. She had her cane chair there, too, and she had sat there, not still and emptily, but mending clothes, sewing on strings and buttons and letting out hems... She thought of that hubbub and of how she had managed and how everyone had said, pretending to think she couldn't hear but really wanting her to, "Isn't she splendid? Isn't she like a queen?" (17-18)..

Through the busy years Nanda had cultivated a privacy of the mind, a 'stillness' and 'composure,' almost an imitation of death. To this sacred precinct of the self, nobody entered. And thus, she had attended to the jobs, had entertained her husband's visitors, had sent many children to schools and colleges, provided for her mother-in-law and innumerable house guests, while inwardly the refrain persisted, "Discharge me . . . I've discharged all my duties."(30)

The 'discharge' comes only with widowhood but her 'radiantly single life' is of short duration, for Nanda Kaul, absorbed in her false notions of freedom, is quickly reminded of her traditional place in the extended family. She is expected to host her great-grand-daughter Raka indefinitely. That Nanda accepts this responsibility, this unwritten obligation to the amorphous Indian family, places Nanda Kaul firmly within the patterns evident in the early twentieth century women's memorablia cited already. For her, duties before personal desires, even though the self-given verdict is accepted in "distress and agitation" (31).

A variation on the same theme are the chapters pertaining to Ila Das whom Nanda describes as a person "who had followed her out of the past and still came to see her" (36). Just as Anita Desai alludes to one kind of feminism in her portrait of Nanda Kaul, another kind of feminine destiny is seen to shape Ila Das. The social-historical context is similar: the women have known each other in childhood, and intermittently, during their adult years. Their childhood harkens back to the late colonial period, the era of borrowed 'gentility' for a few 'privileged' Indians:

> Nanda Kaul's family had known Illa Das's in the days when some of the glory of the British Empire was allowed to reflect on a few favoured natives. Such families lived in large bungalows on quiet roads. In their houses, sherry was served before lunch, port after. Their servants wore white cotton gloves. The ladies went for evening drives along the river, at first in creaking carriages, later in prompously purring automobiles. (110)

Along with this spurious imitation of 'British' lifestyles, went a futile education distancing young Indian girls from their own heritage and offering no viable alternative. What Anita Desai places in the reminiscences of Ill and Nanda is a veiled critique of a fashionable upbringing which left women incapable of dealing with real problems:

> 'Isn't it absurd,' (Ila) rattled on, 'how helpless our upbringing made us, Nanda. We thought we were being equipped with the very best—French lessons, piano lessons, English governesses—my, all that only to find it left us helpless, positively *handicapped*'(127).

Abbreviated here is the outcome of a lengthy debate in social history about the relevance of 'western' education for upper class Hindu girls.[16] Although the origins of the debate were in missionary activities in nineteenth century Bengal, the issues were still sparking controversy in the next century among educationists as well as those who looked to the well-being of their immediate family. Thus Jogesachandra Ghosh's thoughts on *The Daughter of Hindustan* (1928), written from the standpoint of an orthodox paternal figure imbued with the worry of finding appropriate education for 'Hindu' girls, decries the sad situation where Sanskrit schools are too rigid and missionary schools too eclectic in their curricula.[17] Speaking of convent education, Ghosh's view is that "Far from being taught to cherish the Hindu ideals of life, a girl leaving such an institution carries ideas which embarrass her in life and often make her doubt the worth of the sentiments the Hindus so much cherish."[18]

What Nanda Kaul and Ila Das receive as education has the vestiges of the process described by Ghosh. In Ila Das, the woman who was brought up in the imitative gentility of upper class Indians and who then had to earn her livelihood because of decaying family fortunes, Anita Desai has encapsulated the history of a recognisable feminist position. Ila's first job is as a teacher of Home Science in the same university where Nanda's husband is the vice-chancellor. It is amply clear that a friend's compassion rather than formal education has made the appointment possible. Somewhere in the background of this episode is the call for making women's education relevant to their needs, a particular instance of which was the introduction of Home Science as a degree course.[19] As a university teacher, Ila is still in a cultural enclave separate from the poverty, squalor and superstition which brand the Indian masses. Ila's decision to leave teaching and turn to social work marks a significant change from a job to a vocation, and a corresponding transition from a protected middle-class life to direct contact with the poor and their modes of thought.

The futility of Ila's education in circumstances that surround her in Kasauli is tragically conveyed in the story of her attempt to stop a child-marriage. Preet Singh wishes to marry his seven year old daughter to an old widower with six children because "he owns a quarter of an acre of land and two goats." (130) Ila tries to uphold "the law of the land" and threatens Preet Singh with imprisonment "for committing a social offence."[20] Yet, it becomes apparent that the law of the land is respected only by those who believe in it, or fear it, that is the urban middle-class. The remote communities live by customary practices of their own and one of these is child-marriage. Ila's city education and beliefs pose a threat to a community entirely different from her. The villagers know only one solution to the problem—the ancient one of taking justice into their own hands and 'punishing' Ila Das as only a woman can be punished. On a dark evening, Ila is attacked by Preet Singh, strangled, raped and cast away among the pine trees and blue hydrangeas of the Kasauli hills.

Summarizing on the basis of the discussion so far, one may say that Nanda Kaul and Ila Das represent two attitudes of feminism within a historical context which the novel occasionally glances at. Brought up within the tradition of upper-middle class Indian homes in the late colonial period, the women were recipients of European ideas through English education, but these ideas were imperfectly assimilated and often in conflict with the actual business of living in the Indian milieu. Hence Nanda, intellectually alert, dreams of a possible future when she will be 'discharged' from domesticity and left free to pursue her own thoughts. Ila, pushed by circumstances into earning her keep learns of her terrible dissociation from Indian concerns.

These two portraits of feminine options are not limited by their historical context but continue to be relevant in the present times. However, a new current has been introduced, that of radical feminism—energetic, bold, and destructive of traditon. This mood is reflected in Raka, the great-grand-daughter of Nanda Kaul, who has no use for household ritual, would rather explore the Kasauli hills and peer into the club to satisfy her ever-increasing curiosity about her encinrment, and who, in a final burst of anarchic energy, sets the forest on fire.

Within the scheme I have suggested for the novel, Raka is a figure of latent, incipient feminism—hence depicted as a child—intuitive, awkward, and yet, confident. Described by the novelist as "an impatient kernel, small and explosive" (91), she carries the potential for creation as well as disaster. Nanda's first assessment of the child as a timid creature, as "one of those dark crickets that leap up in fright but do not sing, or a mosquito, minute and fine, on thin, precarious legs" (39), changes later to a realization that the child has a mind of her own and a rare "gift of avoiding what she regarded as dispensable" (63).

One of the dispensables in Raka's scheme of things is a boarding school, denoting an unacceptable "discipline, order and obedience" (59); another is the ritual of the tea table, "that game of old age" that Nanda and Ila play at by "reconstructing, block by gilded block, of the castle of childhood" (116). Yet another of Raka's rejections is the social 'past' reconstructed foolishly in the

Fire on the Mountain

Kasauli club. She stares aghast at the costume ball in which men and women dressed as beasts and monsters seem to have undergone a macabre transformation of their human self. What Raka perceives is the general debasement of old customs. The rejections of Raka gather together many scattered strands of the novel. The old forms of education, useless to Nanda and Ila, continue to be practised. In her contemplative moods Nanda acknowledges the worthlessness of the old domestic rituals; yet she surrenders to them by force of habit; moreover, the colonial past persistently casts a long and distorted shadow upon institutions such as the Kasauli club.

Having questioned the acceptances of many generations of women, what is the new feminist's position? By Vina Mazumdar's assessment of the condition of Indian women:

> All the conventional indicators of social change point to the operation of some remorseless forces that are reducing the large majority of our women to greater insecurity, degradation, and helplessness... It seems that while the processes of social change have removed many of the inbuilt protections that traditional society provided to its women... we have failed to replace them by modern institutions of social security.[21]

Hence, the feminist's sense of bewilderment, a desire to act and yet uncertainty about what the mode of expression ought to be. Raka's lineage, both personal and historical, is from Nanda Kaul, and the startling resemblance of the two persons is stated in Anita Desai's words:

> Nanda Kaul saw that she (Raka) was the finished, perfect model of what Nanda Kaul herself was, merely a brave, flawed experiment... .

If Nanda was recluse out of vengeance for a long life of duty and obligation, her great-grand-daughter was a recluse by nature, by instinct (47-48). The difference between them lies in the efficacy of the historical moment, the cataclysmic 'now' when feminists will take a stand.

But to what end one knows not— no more than does Raka, when by some mysterious urge to see the holocaust on the hillside, she sets the dry woods ablaze. Perhaps this is a symbolic burning of "the safe, cosy, civilized world in which Raka had no part and to which she owed no attachment" (91), perhaps this is the only way the child perceives of destroying all that is suggested by isolated cottages, defunct clubs, snake infested and smoking kilns of scientific institutes.[22] In other words, the will to destroy makes no value judgements about what is conducive or harmful to human existence. An extreme position no doubt, and one which gives an unsatisfactory finality to the notion of incipient feminism in Desai's portrayal of the child, Raka.

Darshan Singh Maini had once remarked that Anita Desai is "somehow unable to invent events and episodes that may bring out the dramatic potential of her *donnees*."[23] And indeed, the conclusion of *Fire on the*

Mountain turns attention away from the large social issues the novel is capable of evoking to the more literary issue of Desai's depictions of female neurosis. Critics have amply examined the psychological ploys and there is very little to add. Examined for its sociology, however, *Fire on the Mountain* holds a pivotal position in Desai's corpus of fiction because the three feminist attitudes I have identified can serve as points of reference for several characters in her other novels.

This may be illustrated by a few representative examples. Sita, the protagonist of *Where Shall We Go this Summer?*, goes into a paranoia of distress after knowing of her fifth pregnancy. Rejecting the 'empty shell' of her Bombay apartment, she tries to find peace in the island home of her childhood, praying all the while for 'the miracle of keeping her baby unborn.' Later, realizing the impracticability of her dreams, Sita returns to the mundane routine of Bombay. In as much that Sita's rebellion against social expectation is personal and theoretical, and that she lacks the energy to assert her preferred independence, her similarity with Nanda Kaul is obvious. Marital relationships and the complexities of parental roles, examinded through Monisha's ruminations in *Voices in the City*, again bring out aspects of theoretical, inward-turning feminism. A variation to this theme is the single woman compelled by circumstances to support herself economically without adequate preparation for such a life—the Ila Das figure. Her parallel may be seen in Desai's portrait of Bim (*Clear Light of Day*) who tries to run her father's insurance business and 'dedicates' her life, unwittingly, to the care of the aged and the infirm.

That a parallel to Raka is difficult to find leads me to a speculation about a pattern in Desai's approach to women. The destructive principal is latent in Maya, the self-haunted protagonist of Desai's first novel, *Cry the Peacock* (1963), and Maya fulfils her nature by hurling Gautama from the roof. Monisha, the central character in Desai's next novel, *Voices in the City* (1968) turns the violence against herself and commits suicide. Sita, from a novel of Desai's middle period, *Where Shall We Go This Summer?* (1975) almost contemplates violence against her unborn child. And Raka, as we have seen, sets fire to the hillside and violates nature itself. Beyond this ever-increasing surge of destruction there is only a 'nothingness' for society, and within it, for women. Desai's recent novel *The Village by the Sea* takes the Indian experience to its rural roots, to a fishing village where several children and child-like people are supportive of one another. The village is adjusting to the disruptive forces of new industrialism. The pervading philosphy of the novel, perhaps Desai's own, is in the concluding remark of the bird-watcher to Hari, "Adapt—that is what you are going to do. Just as birds and animals must do if they are going to survive."

The survival is, undoubtedly, in a social context and achieved at the cost of the individual's innate desires if they happen to contradict society. This philosophy of resignation in Desai's late novel, of survival through adaptation, not radical action, offers a gloss on the potentials of feminism suggested in *Fire on the Mountain*. And it is these 'potentials' and 'suggestions' that I wish to relate to my opening statement on the 'conceptual richness' of Desai's novel. Anita Desai's theoretical statements on women's issues—on the social and historical determinants of literature and the creative impulse of women writers are thought provoking and forceful. Indeed, the feminist attitudes, depicted through complex figures, are often lost in the trivial details of existence that Desai insists upon. *Fire on the Mountain* is a case in point. The weight of historical and biographical sources that I have referred to may seem rather heavy for a book of slender proportions and one in which the writer seems reluctant to carry any single idea through. Yet, the approach through feminism opens the novel to a line of analysis which sees an Indian-English novel, in fact a novel about Indian women, in its right sociological perspective. This, in a way, is an elaboration of Desai's own concern with the methods of expression used by Indian women writers: "Writing fiction has become synonymous with living in an ivory tower, a form of escapism. Few will admit that far from being an escape from life, from experience, it is the distillation, the essence of all life and experience."[24] If this desirable 'distillation' leads to symbolism—as happens frequently in Desai's fiction—then I would say it is a mere reworking of a heritage of literature. Nevertheless, if Desai can be seen to project, however obliquely, however discontinuously, the 'essence' of the life and experience of women in their societal identity, then the novels stand within a much richer frame of reference.

Notes

1. The proceedings of the Symposium have been published as *The Eye of the Beholder,* edited by Maggie Butcher, Commonwealth Institute, London, 1983. Anita Desai's paper, entitled "Indian Women Writers" is included.
2. Desai, "Indian Women Writers." *The Eye of the Beholder,* pp. 55-56.
3. *Ibid.*, p. 56.
4. R.S. Sharma, *Anita Desai,* Arnold-Heinemann, New Delhi, 1982, p. 14.
5. Madhusudan Prasad, *Anita Desai: The Novelist,* New Horizon, Allahabad, 1981, p. 142.
6. Desai won the 1978 National Academy of Letters Award for *Fire on the Mountain. Clear Light of Day* and *In Custody* were nominated for the Booker Prize.
7. *The Eye of the Beholder,* p. 58.
8. Page numbers in parenthesis refer to *Fire on the Mountain,* 1977, rpt. Penguin Books, England, 1981. Subsequent references are to the same edition.
9. Public statements on the issues were made by Sarojini

Naidu and Annie Besant. Naidu, "The true standard of a country's greatness lies... in the undying spiritual ideals of love and service and sacrifice that inspired and sustained the mothers of the "Race." G.A Natesan, ed., *Speeches and Writings of Sarojini Naidu,* Madras, 1925, p. 16. Besant, "For India's uplift, her daughters must come out from their seclusion and take back their place in the common life." *The Besant Spirit,* The Theosophical Society, Madras, 1939, p. 115.

10. *A Pattern of Life: The Memoirs of an Indian Woman,* is a fascinating account of Sudha Mazumdar's life as told to the editor Geraldine H. Forbes, Manohar, New Delhi, 1977.
11. *Ibid.,* p. 205.
12. Hansa Mehta, *Indian Women,* is a collection of Mehta's writings, and speeches published by Butala & Co., Delhi, Baroda, 1981..
13. *Ibid.,* p. 46.
14. *Ibid., P. 42.*
15. *Ibid.,* p. 46.
16. This is a special problem in sociology and literature. See Rama Mehta, *The Western Educated Hindu Woman,* Asia Publishing House, Bombay, 1970.
17. Jogesachandra Ghosh, *The Daughter of Hindustan,* 1928, Now rpt., as *Hindu Woman of India,* Bimla Publishing House, Delhi, 1982.
18. *Ibid.,* p. 133.

19. Recall Hansa Mehta's advocacy of Home Science: "Motherhood is considered the greatest function of women. knowledge of mothercraft is necessary." *Indian Women*, p. 46.
20. *The Child Marriage Restraint Act*, 1929, proclaimed the minimum marriageable age for women as 14 and men as 18.
21. Vina Mazumdar, "Status of Women in India," *Demography India*, Vol. IV. 2, 1975, pp. 263-64.
22. Critics have read many meanings into Raka's act of setting the forest on fire. Madhusudan Prasad notes the frequent use of the forest fire as "symbolic of an impending tragedy." See *Anita Desai the Novelist*, pp. 93-94. According to R.S. Sharma, the fire is "expressive of Raka's resolve to destroy a world where a woman cannot hope to be happy without being unnatural," See *Anita Deasi*. p. 127.
23. "The Achievement of Anita Desai." *Indo-English Literature: A Collection of Critical Essays*, ed. K.K. Sharma, Vimal Prakashan, Ghaziabad, 1977, p. 229.
24. *The Eye of the Beholder*, p. 57.

Notes on the Contributors

1. **R.K. Dhawan** teaches English at Shaheed Bhagat Singh College, University of Delhi. He has an M. Litt. in Comparative Literature and Ph.D. on the fiction of Joseph Conrad. In 1979, he studied at Oxford as a British Council scholar. Dr. Dhawan has contributed papers to journals in India and abroad and his articles have recently appeared in critical anthologies. Also, he has edited *Explorations in Modern Indo-English Fiction* and *Henry David Thoreau*. Currently, he is engaged in a U.G.C.—aided project in comparative literature encompassing Indo-English fiction.

2. **N.K. Jain** teaches English at the School of Correspondence Courses of the University of Delhi. He has edited University text books for Indian students.

3. **Prafulla Kar** is a now the Deputy Director of the American Studies Research Centre Hyderabad. He has a Ph.D. in English from the University of Utah. He wrote his dissertation on the novels of Saul Bellow. He was a Reader in English at Utkal University, Bhubaneswar, before joining the ASRC.

4. **Malashri Lal** is Reader in English at the University of Delhi, and has earlier taught at Kanoria College, Jaipur, and Jesus and Mary College, New Delhi. A pre-doctoral

Fulbright Scholar at Harvard (1978-79) and an International Fellow of the American Association of University Women (1978-79), she wrote her doctoral dissertation on "The Concept of Romance in the Major Works of Henry James." She has published articles on Henry James, Ernest Hemingway, and the American Theatre of Protest; has an article forthcoming on Indian Women Novelists in a volume on "Concepts of Feminism" to be published by the Hawaii University Press; and during 1982 assisted Leon Edel in his edition of the Letters of Henry James.

5. **Devinder Mohan** is Reader in the department of English, Punjab University, Chandigarh. He got his Ph.D. from the University of California and has published in scholarly journals in India and abroad.

6. **N.S. Pradhan** is the Principal of Kirori Mal College, Delhi. He has earlier taught English at Khalsa College, Delhi, been a Fulbright scholar at Utah (1969-70), and a Fellow of the American Council of Learned Societies at the University of Michigan, Ann Arbor (1980-81). Author of *Modern American Drama* (New Delhi: Arnold-Heinemann, 1978), he has co-edited *Studies in American Literature* (New Delhi: Oxford University Press, 1976), and edited, with introduction and notes for Indian students, *Death of a Salesman* (1979), *A Doll's House* (1981), *Billy Budd* (1982) and *Desire Under the Elms* (1982). He has published a number of articles and book-reviews on American Literature and on Indian Writing in English in various journals.

Notes on the Contributors

7. **Suresh Raichura** teaches English at Kirori Mal College, University of Delhi. He has studied at New York University on a Fulbright scholarship. He has published a number of articles and book reviews in scholarly journals. He has now completed his dissertation on Jewish American Fiction.

8. **Vasant A. Shahane** is Professor Emeritus in English at Osmania University, Hydrabad. With a doctorate from the University of Leeds, Prof. Shahane has a distinguished record of research and scholarship. He has published books on E.M. Forster, Khushwant Singh, Rudyard Kipling, Ruth P. Jhabvala and has edited several books. He has published more than a hundred articles and reviews in scholarly journals in India and abroad.

9. **Brijraj Singh** is professor in the department of English, University of Delhi. He has previously taught at St. Stephen's College, Delhi, and at North-Eastern Hill University, Shillong. Winner of a Rhodes scholarship in 1962, he got his M.A. from Oxford University, and later as a Fulbright scholar he got his doctorate from Yale University. Brijraj Singh is the author of *Milton, An Introduction, The Development of A Critical Tradition* and has published articles and reviews in Indian and foreign journals.

10. **Lakhmir Singh** teaches English at S.G.T.B. Khalsa College, University of Delhi. He has published a large number of articles and book reviews, several of them being on contemporary Punjabi writers.

11. Ramesh K. Srivastava is Reader in English at Guru Nanak Dev University, Amritsar (Punjab). He got his Ph.D from the University of Utah, U.S.A. He has published a number of short stories and critical articles in English in *Thought, Caravan, Indian Journal of English Studies, Journal of Indian Writing in English, Indian Scholar* and *Punjab Journal of English Studies*. His other publications are: *Determinism in Hemingway, Hemingway and his For Whom the Bell Tolls, Perspectives on Bhabani Bhattacharya,* and *Perspectives on Anita Desai*. He has edited Thoreau's *Walden* for Oxford University Press, Delhi.

12. Harish Trivedi is Reader in English at the University of Delhi, and has earlier taught at the University of Allahabad, the Banaras Hindu University, and St. Stephen's College, Delhi. He was a Commonwealth scholar at the University of Wales (1971-75), and wrote his doctoral dissertation on 'Virginia Woolf and the Tradition of the English Novel.' He has co-edited *Heritage of English* (New Delhi: Macmillan, 1980) and translated from the Hindi *Premchand: A Life (New Delhi:* People's Publishing House, 1982). He has also edited *The American Political Novel* (New Delhi: Allied Publishers, 1984).